MW00472629

HOW TO SELF-PUBLISH A BOOK

FOR THE TECHNOLOGY CHALLENGED AUTHOR

BARB DROZDOWICH

Copyright © 2018 by Barb Drozdowich

All rights reserved.

No part of this book may be reproduced in any form or by any electronic
or mechanical means, including information storage and retrieval systems,
without written permission from the author, except for the use of brief
quotations in a book review.

❀ Created with Vellum

I would like to thank you for buying one of my books!

I tend to focus on the technical tasks that authors and bloggers need to learn. As of this publishing I have 17 books in print and several more in various stages of completion. I'm always looking to be helpful - often creating books around subjects that I get a lot of questions on from authors and bloggers just like you.

At the end of this book is the link join my group of readers and get some free help with the technical subjects.

On to the book - I hope you enjoy and learn lots!

CONTENTS

Introduction   ix

Part I
FOUNDATION SUBJECTS
1. Foundations   3
2. What is Modern Publishing?   13
3. E-Readers   23
4. Structure of a Book   29

Part II
THE BASICS
5. Roadmap/Flowchart   37
6. Editing   41
7. ISBNs   53
8. Cover Graphic   59

Part III
GETTING THE MANUSCRIPT READY FOR
PUBLISHING
9. Get the Manuscript Ready   71
10. File Formats   75
11. Structure Details of a Book   81
12. Formatting   91

Part IV
WHERE TO SELL YOUR BOOK
13. Where Do You Sell Your Book?   107
14. Book Retailers   109
15. Distributors & Aggregators   121

Part V
HOW TO SET UP ACCOUNTS
16. How to Set up Accounts 133

Part VI
INSTRUCTIONS FOR UPLOADING
17. Instructions for Uploading 139

Part VII
STRATEGIES
18. Strategies 151

Part VIII
AUDIOBOOKS & LOOSE ENDS
19. Audiobooks 161
20. Loose Ends 165

Part IX
SELF-PUBLISHING SERVICES
21. About Self-Publishing Services 171
22. Self-Publishing Services 177

Conclusion 181
Interested in getting more technical help? 183

Part X
APPENDIX
Glossary 187
Chart of Distributors 195
File Requirements 203
What do Editors Do? 207
Bibliography 213
Resources 215
Articles for Further Reading 221
YouTube Videos 225
Writers Groups 227
Sources of Editors 231

About the Author   233
Also by Barb Drozdowich   235
Excerpt from Blogging for Authors   243
Excerpt from The Complete Mailing List ToolKit   249

INTRODUCTION

Self-publishing—or Indie publishing, as it is also known—is the publishing equalizer. Gate-keepers are removed and authors can publish a book they feel has merit. Along with the removal of many of the gate-keepers, in recent years much of the stigma has also been removed. Authors who choose to publish their own work are capable of having a respectable and successful career as published authors.

So...you are interested in learning about self-publishing. Do you use the term "Self-Publishing" or "Indie-Publishing" or "Independent Publishing"? In my mind all these phrases mean the same thing. They all refer to the act of publishing a book where you are the driver of the operation—you may ask for, and receive, help, but you make all the decisions.

I am the proud author of 15 self-published books, have sold thousands of copies and I am frequently answering questions about or dispelling myths about self-publishing. As a result, I decided to put fingers to keyboard and explain the process of self-publishing.

Why self-publishing? Really, aren't there several books

out there that deal with the subject? There are, and I've read most of them. Many of the books available focus on either the US or the UK or don't specify the differences experienced by self-publishers in different countries. That is where this book is different. I will point out the differences and provide as many sources of information I can find for folks in different countries.

Is there a learning curve?
Yes!

I do feel the learning curve is reasonable, but in my experience, many well-meaning people scare authors off this path.

I approach the world of authors and publishing differently than most authors. My background is in teaching science and running a technical training department. I'm a stats geek and I tend to analyze things, to study things. I don't *think* things work, I *know* they do and *why* they do. I read a lot and I research a lot. The origins for most of my books have been either a problem point that I discover or a subject that I get a lot of questions on.

There is no one way to publish a book.

Maybe that's what creates confusion in many authors—the number of choices that exist. As you'll see in this book, I view publishing as steps on a flow chart or as stops on a road map. Steps that are easily identified and described. They are all steps that the average author can carry out— perhaps with a bit of help—but they don't require any special skill other than some patience and a little bit of stubbornness. There are a variety of choices available for most of the steps. We'll talk about the choices available and talk about the pros and cons of each.

I think it's important to let you know what you will learn from this book. We will start off talking about the various types of editing and how to find an editor for your project. We will talk about how to get an ISBN from whatever agency is appropriate for your country. We will talk about what all the various file formats are we will need to publish our book and how to either create them ourselves or how to find a professional formatter. We will learn all about cover graphics and how to find a graphic designer to help create the perfect cover for your book. We will learn how straightforward it is to publish a book to the various retailers where your book will be for sale. We will learn about e-readers and how straightforward they are to use. We will learn about the differences between all the retailers and learn how to get paid. Along the way, we'll learn the meaning of all those words that published authors use that don't seem to be part of the normal English language. We'll learn a bunch of bits and pieces that make the whole thing much easier! And homework. I'll be assigning homework, but it will be fun homework. Think "reading a book" kind of fun.

Lastly, I'll give you lots and lots of help. At the end of this book, you'll find a glossary, a list of resource articles, a list of helpful videos, an extensive list of writers' groups and a few odds and ends of resource material that I just had to include!

Are you excited to begin? I hope so. Let's end this introduction with a quote from a group that I will mention several times in this book—the Alliance of Independent Authors.

"What self-publishing doesn't do is absolve us of the responsibility of learning our craft and our art."
~ Alliance of Independent Authors

I

FOUNDATION SUBJECTS

FOUNDATIONS

I n this chapter, we're going to lay out the foundations for your understanding of the world and the process of self-publishing. Part of the foundation work involves us all speaking the same language. It also involves me helping you see things that you likely didn't pay attention to previously.

You will realize as we progress through the various topics that I like to assign homework. Isn't there a saying about taking the teacher out of the classroom? Regardless… in my experience, homework can be a good thing.

The homework that I assign will have a point to it. In some cases, it will encourage you to step outside of your comfort zone. You see, in my experience when most beginner authors picture their book for sale, they picture a paperback book. The reality, which we'll talk about in a future chapter, is the vast majority of books sold are electronic, not paperback. We'll come back to that topic.

Your first piece of homework relates to paperback books. We all read paperback books, but since we are going to be talking about actually creating one, we need to *really look* at a book.

To that end, grab some paperback books—perhaps from your personal bookshelves—and study some examples. Don't read the books, study them. Look at the information that is in the front and the back of the book (called front and back matter respectively). Look at how the text is laid out on the pages. Look at the chapter starts. Look at the front and back cover. Take some notes about what you like and don't like. Study the commonalities from book to book. Study the differences. We'll come back to this information a bit later.

Before we get very far into the topic of Self-Publishing we need to define some terms and talk about what self-publishing is and what it isn't. As I mentioned previously, as part of the foundations, we need to speak the same language. Over the years words or labels about publishing have been used as weapons by the opposite camp. A self-publishing guide that has been produced by the Alliance of Independent Authors, a group that I belong to, shared the following quote in their book:

> *"Self-publishing evangelists compare traditional publishers to lumbering dinosaurs, incapable of adapting to a changing world. Self-publishing, they say, is the only worthwhile path to freedom and success. Traditional publishing evangelists characterize self-publishing as nothing more than a titanic slush pile, and declare that real credibility is reserved for books that carry the logo of a traditional publishing house. Neither of these views reflects reality, though each holds a grain of truth. In this contentious debate, it's hard to find anyone who hasn't taken a side—which can make things difficult for writers who are searching for unbiased information."*

I wanted to share the above quote as I think that it honestly characterizes the current climate in publishing. In addition to the two deeply divided camps, there is the reality that authors who choose to self-publish are frequently taken advantage of by individuals/companies which count on beginner authors' lack of understanding of the publishing world. We'll talk more about that topic in one of the last chapters of this book, but for now, let's talk about terminology, so that we are all speaking the same language going forward.

Self-publishing: As the dictionary would suggest, if we are going to use the word "self" we are suggesting that all actions are taken by "self" or by the author. This isn't necessarily true, as often this phrase refers to publishing that is directed by the author, but the tasks are not literally done by the author.

Indie-Publishing or Independent Publishing: To go back to the dictionary, this would indicate a form of publishing that is done alone or without the support of a company or corporation to carry out many of the tasks. It can also refer to publishing that takes place outside of the old-school traditional realm. For example, many smaller presses are referred to as Independent Publishers as they are one-person enterprises or small shops.

As I've mentioned, I really don't draw a difference between self-publishing and indie-publishing (independent publishing). Although they are likely the most common terms used to describe the type of publishing we will discuss in this book, the term that I actually prefer is Author-directed Publishing. I like to refer to myself as an Authorpreneur—a term that is gaining popularity in my publishing world.

Let's define some terms that we will use going forward.

Manuscript - is the term that is used to refer to the book that is being worked on. This manuscript is typically in the form of a Microsoft Word document for most of the time this work is being done. Microsoft Word is the industry standard, but other programs can be used to create a manuscript. In fact a manuscript can be created on paper using a pen, but the basis of publishing in the modern era is an electronic file like Word, not paper.

Publishing - is the term that is used to refer to the set of actions that make a book available to the reader. In today's modern era, publishing involves submitting an electronic file to a location where it will be available for sale or to a company that will share it with companies that will sell it to readers.

Let's clarify that last statement a bit. Readers purchase books from **Retailers**. An example of a Retailer may be a bricks-and-mortar business like Chapters/Indigo, Barnes & Noble or Waterstones, but it can also be an online company such as Amazon or Kobo.

Some retailers that sell our books allow authors to submit to them directly. Other retailers are accessed through a middleman. That middleman may be called an aggregator or a distributor.

We shouldn't confuse the term **publishing** with **printing**. Publishing is the act of making a book available to be purchased by a reader via a retailer. Printing is the act of turning an electronic manuscript into a paper copy. In today's modern era of publishing, as indie authors we can't print a book and make it available for sale in bookstores (other than as a consignment item). We use Print on Demand services attached to retailers to make paper versions of our books available to readers.

As we'll find out in one of the last chapters of this book, many authors see the act of creating physical books to be publishing. It is not. And there are many authors who end up with boxes of their paper books piled up in their home with few places to sell them.

The next word we will define in this section is **Formatting**. This is a term that is liberally thrown around the author world! It, in fact, can mean many things. We say that we "format" our Word document to display the text in specific ways. We "format" it to indent paragraphs, to show chapter titles in a specific way or to display nicely styled quotations. This is true. In the author world, we also use the term "format" to refer to the process of taking a Word document and changing it to make it ready to be accepted by retailers. This type of formatting may be as simple as adding page numbers or as complicated as turning it into another type of file entirely. We will talk about both versions of the word "format" in future chapters.

The last term we need to define in this section is the word **Publisher**. In the indie publishing world, the author is the publisher. The author may create a company and use that company name to display as the publisher of note. The author may hire a small or independent publishing company that will ultimately display as the publisher of note. As I mentioned previously, in the self-publishing or indie-publishing world, the author is the one that drives the boat—who makes all the decisions. Who literally shows as the publisher of note has implications that we will discuss in a future chapter.

Let's move on and talk about some of the other terms that are thrown around in the indie/self-publishing world.

Hybrid Publishing - the term Hybrid Publishing today refers to a type of partnership. This partnership is typically between an author and a small publishing company. If we assume that in traditional publishing, the publisher pays for all costs of publishing and in indie/self-publishing the author pays for all costs, hybrid publishing is somewhere in the middle. Typically a hybrid publishing arrangement is formed when a publishing company is unwilling to pay for and accept all risk for a book, yet is willing to have it available under its publishing umbrella if the author pays for some or all of the costs of production.

Just as an aside, did you realize that an author can be

hybrid also? They can. I love the way Chuck Wendig talks about hybrid authors with this quote:

> The hybrid author merely looks at all the publishing options available to her. She is told she is supposed to check one box and move on — "Stay within the clearly-marked margins," they warn. "Check your box, choose your path, then shut the door gently behind you." But the hybrid author checks many, even *all* the boxes. The hybrid author refuses to walk one path, instead leaping gaily from path to path, gamboling about like some kind of jester-imp. She says no to coloring within the lines of a *traditionally-published* or a *self-published* drawing.
>
> She opens all the doors. She closes none of them.

So let's define a hybrid author as an author who is self-published or traditionally published depending on what suits the project or in fact parts of a project.

Partnership publishing - like hybrid publishing, partnership publishing refers to some sort of agreement or partnership between the author and various service providers. This partnership may be limited or all encompassing. And it typically doesn't refer to an arrangement with an already existing publishing house.

Joint Ventures - another type of collaborative arrangement where authors play various roles, sometimes involving other service providers such as formatters. There are examples of groups of authors joining together to pool their resources and expertise to publish books of various descriptions. An example of this is multi-author box sets.

Collective publishing - this type of publishing often refers to a group working together, sharing skills to get all published. Similar to Joint Ventures, it is not unusual to see groups of authors with various skills collaborating and pooling these skills.

Shared Publishing - similar to Joint Ventures, this term indicates shared responsibility amongst a group of people.

Vanity Publishing – According to my research, the term "vanity publishing" was the earliest iteration of self-publishing. Going back a number of years, the ability for an individual author to upload files and access distributors as we do now simply didn't exist. Many authors who, for one reason or another, decided to not go the traditional publishing route, found a way to publish their own books. Frequently this involved finding a printer to print copies of paperbacks and either selling them on a personal website or on a consignment basis at a neighborhood bookstore. Keep in mind Amazon came onto the book/publishing scene in 1994. Before this and even for some years after this date, e-books really didn't exist as we see them today. Amazon released its first Kindle reader in 2007—only 10 years ago.

Subsidized publishing - this is a term that often applies to projects that are funded by organizations. Often anthologies or poetry collections that are organized and published by writer's groups have the costs paid for by the organization, not the authors' themselves.

Agent assisted self-publishing - this is a new type of self-publishing that has appeared in the last few years. In this situation, an agent who is unable to sell a book to a traditional publisher will help the author through the process of self-publishing and collect a portion of the royalties for their efforts. This is a good thing when it is done with good intentions, but I've heard tales of people describing themselves as agents, convincing authors to pay for all the activities involved in self-publishing, uploading files under their name or ISBN, collecting 15% royalties when there was no chance or effort made to have the book sold to a traditional publisher. Authors who don't understand that the ISBN and ASIN are now in the agent's name and if they leave, they will lose their rankings.

"For those looking to traditionally publish, don't get roped into thinking that if an agent helps you self-publish, you'll have a better chance at reaching traditional publishers with your next manuscript...it is essentially a way for agents to stay afloat in a changing publishing environment..."
~ Melissa Foster, Bestselling Indie Author

Let's be clear about the absolute difference between self/indie-publishing and traditional publishing:

With true traditional publishing, the author pays nothing and gets little in terms of royalties.

With true self-publishing, the author pays all the costs and retains most of the royalties.

A term that is gaining popularity in the publishing world is the term "Legacy Publishing." It is a term used to refer to what many call Traditional Publishing. It is used often to indicate that the big traditional publishers are considered to be old-school by many, dinosaurs by many and gradually disappearing from the marketplace. They have many years, in fact centuries of history in publishing, but many critics don't see a future for them. There are many things the "Big 5 Publishers" do well. They have many years of experience in the publishing arena and have the infrastructure to take on projects that print on demand can't do justice to—like art books, coffee table books, children's pop-up books and the like. But as I said at the beginning of this section, the camps are entrenched and often the positives of both camps are overlooked.

In the coming chapters we will be talking about the various steps—the bits and pieces needed—to publish a book. As I noted previously in this chapter, by "publish a book," I mean have it in a form available for sale to people around the world. We aren't going to limit ourselves to discussing the act of printing a book any more than we will limit ourselves to the act of editing that book. This book will cover the whole enchilada, as the saying goes. We will talk about taking a manuscript, having it edited and revised where needed, creating a cover graphic, formatting it and making it available to the reading public as either an e-book or as print copy or hopefully both.

In the next chapter we are going to talk about what the world of publishing looks like now—in 2018. What publishing looks like for Indie or self-published authors. Stay tuned for more homework and learning new things.

2

WHAT IS MODERN PUBLISHING?

I n my day-to-day dealings with authors I realize that the world of getting a book in front of the eye of readers is a confusing place for many writers and authors. Many grew up in a world where only the big traditional publishers placed books in front of readers. As I said previously, that world is changing. There are still traditional publishers, like Penguin and Hachette, who continue to publish books their way, and many authors coming into this world of modern publishing try to emulate their model. They try to focus on paper books. They try to focus on sales in bookstores. And they try to focus on only local markets.

Today's publishing world is international and it is primarily digital and sales are mostly online. We'll talk about some facts and figures in a bit that back that statement up. However, for those authors trying to emulate what I'll call "old-school publishing," not only is confusion the name of the game, but they often fail to succeed because they aren't aware of the big picture of today's modern publishing.

Common sense would tell us that anyone who is going

to open a store to sell T-shirts would visually inspect those T-shirts to ensure the quality of goods they were selling. This common sense does not continue on to authors selling books. While an author would not hesitate to get a print copy of their book and inspect it, those authors who have not made the leap to reading on an e-reader would not inspect a digital copy of their book. Instead, they simply hope that all is well.

As we go through this book, I assign homework. You may chuckle at the things I suggest you do. Like the exercise from Chapter 1—pick up a paperback book and study it. How many of you actually did that? Or did you read the instructions and think to yourself: "I'm familiar with paper-backs so I don't need to ACTUALLY do this." I have specific reasons for asking you to do various activities. They stem from experience. I know what authors—even experienced ones—are comfortable with. I want to help you step out of that comfort zone and truly understand this modern version of publishing. I want to help you become comfort-able with the tools and language of publishing in 2018.

One of those tools is an e-reader. This is a device to read electronic versions of books. It may be a physical device or it may be an app that has been installed on a phone, tablet, or computer. It may go by the name Kindle, Nook, Kobo reader or Sony reader. It may be an app that is named after a bookstore or a publishing house. The world of e-readers is large and it is varied. It is also a place where a significant number of your readers will read your books. Although we will discuss some details in the next chapter, as an author, you need to be able to, at the very least, visually inspect the product that you are selling to the world.

To this end, let's have another homework assignment! This one attacks the world of e-readers or reading elec-tronic books.

If you don't have an e-reader in the house, now is the time to step in to the electronic world. You will be selling electronic books. Just as if you were selling T-shirts, you want to look at the product you are selling to check for quality. It is easier than you think to do this. You'll need two types of e-reader apps on a device, as there are two basic types of e-readers and we'll learn about these in a future chapter. For now, I want you to go to Amazon and, if you don't already have one, open an account. If you are on a laptop, search for Kindle apps. Find one that is applicable for your computer and download it. If you are doing this exercise on a phone or tablet, you need to go through the appropriate App store. "Buy" a few free books or spend a few dollars and get a few books that interest you. Like you did with the paperback, study the various books. Play with the app, change the settings, change the font size, change the brightness of the screen. See what happens. You can do the same with the Kobo app (from Kobo.com), the Nook app (from Barnes & Noble) or the iBooks app (already installed on all Apple products) These apps read a different format of e-book. Open your Kobo (Barnes & Noble or iBook) app and download some books from Kobo (Nook or iTunes)—free or paid. As with the Kindle app, look at the books, play with the settings, change the font and so on. Take some notes. We will talk about e-readers and e-reader apps in the next chapter.

In the publishing world a lot of numbers are thrown about. Everyone has an opinion as to whether books are selling (or not), and what types of books are selling (or not). Just the other day my local paper ran an article that tried to convince me that e-books are dead. If there are all sorts of numbers circulating that contradict one another, how is an author to determine what reality is?

I'm a self-confessed stats geek. I like to use numbers and stats to guide my actions, especially when talking about publishing. When I found out about "Data Guy," I found someone after my own heart. Not only has "Data Guy" been analyzing and sharing numbers about publishing for a while now, he has spoken at a number of large conferences. And although he has appeared in person at large conferences such as Digital Book World and Romance Writers of America, he doesn't use his real name, but prefers to use his moniker both online and in person. He posts on his website — Author Earnings (http://authorearnings.com) — and focuses his skill with numbers on tracking author earnings.

As I said, numbers and statements are thrown around easily in our publishing world.

"E-books are on the decline."
"Paperbacks are dead."

Which is true? The statements contradict one another so they can't possibly both be true. So let's see what Data Guy has to say about these commonly thrown about lines.

Data Guy analyzes the data that he obtains from the actual retailers—not the publishers—and presents a less biased view of book sales. He has carried out four major recent studies which I'll use numbers from—one in 2016 where he analyzed overall Author Earnings, one from 2016 where he compared Print vs Digital, Traditional vs Non-Traditional, Bookstore vs Online Sales, an analysis that compares more international numbers, and most recently, he studied the 2017 numbers from online sales in the US.

I love this opening quote from the most recent article:

> *"Today, with the click of a button, any author can start selling any title they wish simultaneously in 12 country-specific Amazon stores, 36 country-specific Kobo e-book stores, and over 40 country-specific Apple e-book stores."*

I don't want to bog you down with numbers and stats that I find completely fascinating, instead my intent for this chapter is to help you understand that book sales are not local, they are international; self-publishing is outpacing traditional publishing, and contrary to what many traditional publishers say, e-books sales are outpacing paperback book sales.

Typically, most of the numbers that come out of the publishing world, come from traditional publishers, or organizations that rely on tracking paperback sales. Those are the numbers that are used in articles which claim to know where the publishing world is headed. These numbers completely miss out on e-book sales or non-traditional sales. When Data Guy started to publish results and speak at major conferences, he opened more than a few eyes.

In the first major study that Data Guy published in late 2016, he claimed that on the surface (for 2016), sales for Traditional publishers were as follows:

- Print – 76%
- E-books – 21%
- Audio – 3%

Those numbers clearly indicate that print books rule. But are broad stripes like that meaningful? The answer is: not really. When the overall numbers are broken down into a number of categories, some important details can be seen (while still staying with numbers from traditional publishers):

- 49% of adult fiction sales are digital sales
- 24% of adult non-fiction sales are digital
- 12% of juvenile fiction sales are digital
- 6% of juvenile nonfiction sales are digital

That's kind of striking, isn't it? Almost a half of all sales of traditionally published books are digital copies—e-books and audio books. The numbers are a bit different when talking about books for the younger set.

The next question that was asked was where are the sales happening? Many of us have fond memories of wandering the aisles of bookstores in search of our next read. However, the numbers show that 41% of all tradition-ally published print books sold in the US are purchased online. To add more detail by parsing out the genre groups we find that:

- 63% of adult fiction is bought online
- 69% of adult non-fiction is bought online
- 40% of juvenile fiction is bought online
- 41% of juvenile nonfiction is bought online

Now that we've had a peek at the world of traditional publishers, we need to bring non-traditional publishing numbers into the mix. If you remember from the beginning, these are some of the numbers that are not included when "the E-book is on the decline" comments are made by the press. The non-traditional publishing industry represents a $1.25 billion-dollar industry in the US. What is non-tradi-tional? It is made up of small – mid-sized publishers, indie publishers and Amazon imprints.

When those numbers are added in, we find out that 42% of Adult Fiction sales are of non-traditional titles. In fact, when the non-traditional publishers are added in, we find that 70% of all adult fiction sales are digital—e-book and audio—and 77% of all adult fiction sales are online.

When we look at total sales online—Traditional and non-traditional—the numbers are striking:

- 45% juvenile nonfiction purchased online
- 48% juvenile fiction purchased online
- 72% adult nonfiction purchased online
- 77% adult fiction purchased online

Clearly there is some difference between adult and juvenile purchases. In fact if the groups are further subdivided by genres, huge differences are seen. With the cumulative data that Data Guy has, he has the ability to start to show trends of where book buying dollars are spent. When talking about book sales overall, he shows us they are moving more and more online, and when talking about adult fiction and nonfiction, the numbers are more dramatic.

Let's move on to talk about numbers that include non-US sales. Although most authors show the vast majority of their sales from the US and UK markets—acknowledged to be the largest markets —what happens in other markets?

According to Data Guy's study of sales in the top English-speaking markets, he shares some information about non-US buying habits. Let's start with Canadians: Canadians (in 2017) spent 180 million dollars on books and this money bought 26,017,000 e-books and 50,500,000 print books. Doing the math, about 34% of purchases were e-books. Canadians spend their e-book dollars as follows:

- Amazon – 52%

- Apple – 17%
- Kobo – 27.3%
- Other/GooglePlay – 3.7%

Let's move on to some UK numbers: Folks who shop at the UK versions of the various online retailers spend almost $96M a year in e-Book - about 34% of total book sales. The numbers amongst the retailers break down as follows:

- Amazon - 87.9%
- Apple - 7.5%
- Other - 2.0%
- GooglePlay - 1.2%

Let's move from here to Australia — what is considered to be the 4th largest market studied by Data Guy. In Australia they spent about $22M on e-books, which accounts for about 28% of total sales. The numbers amongst the retailers are as follows:

- Amazon - 60.6%
- Apple - 29.8%
- Kobo - 6.2%
- Other - 2.0%

Everybody shops at Amazon! The percentages from Apple, Kobo, GooglePlay and "Other" vary from country to country, however Amazon is primary source of sales in every country Data Guy studied.

Self-publishing or indie publishing is popular in every

country studied with somewhere between 27% and 45% of all e-book sale dollars going to indie/self-published authors.

Let's bring a conclusion to what we've learned.

- As time goes on, more and more sales of books are moving to an online venue
- In the US as much as 77% of all adult fiction and 72% of all adult nonfiction is purchased online
- In non US countries, between 28% and 34% of all book purchases are carried out online—likely more as those numbers are only the e-book numbers
- Bricks & Mortar locations continue to drop in importance as points of sale

So, why do we care? First and foremost, remember the ideal of most beginner authors of selling their books in a bookstore? The numbers prove that isn't likely to be true. They also show that publishing a book online through Amazon and the like, depending on what genre is written, is likely the primary point of sales.

If we come back to the quote from the beginning of the chapter, with the click of a button, authors can be selling their books in a large range of countries within minutes.

This quote continues with:

"...the global e-book marketplace is a seamlessly international one.

For authors, selling an e-book to a reader in a different country is just as easy as selling to a reader in your home country. Barriers to reaching an international audience no longer exist."

And lastly, Data Guy weighs in on the "Indie Market" when he says:

"... readers see a single holistic e-book market in which titles are NOT at all differentiated by:
– size of publisher
— name of publisher
– or even whether a title was self-published or used any traditional publisher at all

So I'd opine that there's no such thing as an "indie e-book market" per se, only the current indie share of the overall e-book market—a share that indies, by competing more and more effectively, have the power to grow."

I'll leave you with those thoughts as we move on to the topic of e-readers.

3

E-READERS

In my experience many writers are purists. They like the feel of a paper book in their hands. They like the smell of a new book. They could spend many happy hours wandering the aisles of their local bookstore. When they picture their book published, they picture a paper book on the shelves of that local bookstore.

Reality tells us the books we sell will be in a number of formats. Yes, some will be paperback (and perhaps hard cover) but likely the vast majority will be electronic copies. Data Guy's stats, which we talked about in the previous chapter, prove this with real numbers. Since many writers I work with are purists, they are often completely confused by the world of electronic books. However, since you will be selling these types of books, not only should you understand how to proof your final copy, you should also understand the various products out there available to read your book on.

In the next chapter, I'll talk about the various file types that you'll need in the process of "publishing" but for now we are going to talk about the various ways that electronic books can be read.

The electronic book world is basically divided into Amazon/Kindle and all the rest. The book that is read on a Kindle or a device from Amazon is one file type and every other retailer uses a different file type. That fact will give you a leg up on the next chapter, but it also lets you know that any book purchased from Amazon must be read on an Amazon product. Yes, there are ways around this, but for our purposes in this book we will accept that as fact.

Most of us are familiar with Amazon, but have you read a book on a Kindle or a Kindle app? As I said at the beginning of this chapter, even if you don't intend to regularly be a proponent of e-readers, you need to approve the product that you will be selling to customers. I've made the equivalency to T-shirts in a previous chapter. Most of us would accept scrutinizing a physical product, like a T-shirt, if that is what we are selling, but hesitate to look at an e-book because the medium is unfamiliar. That needs to change. We need to learn to walk confidently in the world of our readers!

Manipulating the settings on an e-reader

If you don't have a Kindle reader or a Kindle app on your computer, tablet or phone, let's start there. On your computer go to Amazon and search for "Kindle App." You'll be brought to a screen that offers you choices for downloading an app depending on the device you are using. If you are on a laptop or desktop, choose to download the applicable copy. If you are on a phone or tablet, your app will be obtained from the Mac App Store or GooglePlay Store. You'll likely have to sign into your Amazon account. (If you don't have an Amazon account, now is a great time to start.) As soon as you log into your Amazon account, your app will be connected to your Amazon account.

Now, go forth and find some books. If you are on a tight budget, look through the free selections. "Buy" a couple of books, fix yourself a beverage and find a comfy chair and play with your new reading device. Your new books will have been delivered to your Kindle or Kindle App and be ready to be read. All Kindles and Kindle apps have the ability to change the settings in a variety of ways. The font, font size, line spacing, font color and even the lightness of the background are among the things that can be changed. At the end of a long day of working on a computer, my eyes are tired. One of the main reasons I like reading on my Kindle app on my iPad is I can take my glasses off, increase the font size and read in comfort. Not something I can do with a paperback unless I purchase a large print edition.

Why this exercise?

The reason that I have you go through the exercise of playing with the settings is to help you understand that e-books are intrinsically different than paper books. Their text is fluid, while the text in a paper book is static or frozen. There will be some features that don't change regardless of what you do with the settings. For example, you will notice that there is no setting for images. Tap or click your way through a couple of books. Note the headers or footers (text and/or numbers at the top and bottom of the pages), note whether there are page numbers or location indications, note what the chapter starts look like.

You notice that headers/footers and chapter starts don't really change but there are typically no page numbers, as the number of pages will change with the size of the font and the size of the screen. Play with the font size and see what it does to the location numbers (or percentage read) at the bottom of the screen.

Depending on whether you are playing on a Kindle device like a Kindle Paperwhite or a Kindle Fire, or an app on a desktop computer or tablet, you may or may not be able to see color. The basic Kindle readers have what's called iInk and it is meant to mimic a paperback book in terms of the reading experience. The screen isn't backlit and there is no color capability. Any pictures or graphics that are part of the book will be seen in greyscale. If, however, you are using a Kindle App on a desktop computer or tablet, you likely have color capabilities, as the app will draw on the color capabilities of the device.

Again, this information is to help you understand the reading environment of your readers. In one of my first books I referred to button color and link colors in the color graphics that were included as part of the book. It wasn't until I won a Kindle Paperwhite in a giveaway that I realized that color isn't always seen. My excitement over my book with 200+ color images died a quiet death of embarrassment when I realized this. You see, I did proof my book on my Kindle App on my iPad—full color capability—it never occurred to me to look further.

Let's move on to other types of e-readers. Because I live in Canada, I'm fairly familiar with Kobo readers or Kobo reading app. However, as I pointed out in a previous chapter, there are other choices of e-readers that may or may not be popular in your country. If you are in the US, have a look at the Nook reader or Nook app which should be available from the US iTunes app store. You may also want to look at the iBook app that is already installed on your iPhone, iPad or other Apple product.

Whichever product you decide to play with, go to the

online location and open a free account. If you are going to test out Kobo, go to Kobo.com, if you are going to test out the Nook app, go to BN.com, etc. Once you have an account and have logged into that account through the device or app that you have decided to play with, search through the available books. Buy a few books. If you are on a budget, search through the free books and "buy" a few. They should be automatically delivered to your device or app. Go through the same exercise as you did with a Kindle. Find the settings controls—on the app they are likely in the upper right—and play with what's available. See what you can do to the font, font size, spacing and so on. Study the choices of books and what the pages, chapter starts, headers, footers, etc. look like.

If you are "lucky" in your choices of books you will get yourself some really bad examples of how books should look on an e-reader. To a large degree, an e-book should resemble a paper book in several ways. Typically it has headers that remind you what book you are reading, and perhaps the author name. The chapter starts should have text that begins partway down the screen, not jammed up against the top. Pages shouldn't run into one another just because the pages are now screens. For example, the copyright page shouldn't share space with a Dedication or Table of Contents. In fact, Amazon requires all books, fiction or non-fiction to have a working TOC (Table of Contents)—but more about that in the section on formatting.

There are other e-readers you may or may not have access to. If you have any Apple product from an iPhone to a desktop computer, it will have come equipped with iBooks—the reading app from iTunes. This app will be connected to your iTunes account and will read any iBook. A free reading program that is available from Adobe is Digital Editions and is available for PCs and Macs. This is a good item to have on your computer to easily load up pre-published books to quickly check for issues.

A frustrating feature about the e-book world is the number of apps and programs available to read on. Every store that offers e-books for sale has an app/device or program. Barnes & Noble has the Nook app and Nook e-reader. We have mentioned what Kobo, iTunes, Google Play and Amazon have to offer. Many of the more minor retailers have gotten in on the game—and so have the publishers. I personally have a Harper Collins app on my tablet. A quick search of the Mac App store or Google Play store will show a large selection of independent reading apps. This quantity of e-readers (or apps) can create confusion, not only amongst readers. In my experience, readers tend to be tied to one retailer for their e-books. I think this is primarily so that all their e-books are in one location on their computer/tablet/phone.

I hope this review has opened your eyes, perhaps taught you a few things that you didn't know. In the next chapter we are going to talk about the parts and pieces that make up the structure of a book.

4

STRUCTURE OF A BOOK

Books have been published for centuries. The structure of a book hasn't changed for a really long time. In this chapter we're going to be talking about what goes where—the order of the pages and the placement of the text on the page.

If you remember, one of your first bits of homework was to pick up some paperback books and study them. In this chapter we are going to talk about the traditional parts of a book—what you likely saw when you studied some books. What makes up the front matter, what is included in the body, and what makes up the back matter. As an indie author, you will be putting most of this information together either before sending your manuscript off to your editor or after. Because this is standard structural information about a book, I'm including it in our Foundations section, but this content will be referred to in later sections of this book.

Writers often try to let their creativity show in the structure of their book. There are many places writers can let their creativity shine through, but the structure isn't the best place for a number of reasons.

I'm a Science student and I'm always researching things. Study after study shows that humans like "normal" or "usual" or "expected." This plays out in many different arenas, but when talking about books, adults (and even kids) are familiar with the structure of a book. We know where the title page is; we know where to find the TOC (table of contents); we know what paragraphs and chapters should look like. You should aim to create a product that is as close to "normal" as you can get it to avoid throwing off your audience. The second reason to keep the structure of your book fitting within norms is Amazon as well as other retailers will actually have rules around the structure of a book. More on that in a future chapter.

"When authors decide to format their own books, they don't always make the best choices. It's important to stay within formatting conventions because printed books have existed for a long while. Longstanding habits of readers and accepted trade practices have come to dictate that we follow these formatting guides unless we have a pretty good reason not to."

Joel Friedlander - The Book Designer

(https://www.thebookdesigner.com/2013/08/book-layouts-page-margins/)

Page and Section order

Let's start with the order of the pages or the order of sections of a book. Perhaps before we start, grab a paperback book you own and thumb through the pages to refresh your memory of what's there. There will be content in the front of the book before the story starts, there will be the pages that hold the story and there will be pages in the back after the story is finished. Let's call these sections, Front matter, Body and Back matter.

A) **Front matter** pages are traditionally numbered with lowercase Roman Numerals and contain some or all of the following:

1) **Title Page** - contains information about the title, subtitle or tagline, author and publisher. It is common to put the logo and location of the publisher on the bottom half of this page. This page typically has no number.

2) **Copyright Page** - this page is usually on the back side of the title page and will contain some or all of the following: copyright notice, edition information, cataloging information, ISBN and/or CIP number. There may also be notes of credit for various members of your team—the editor, cover designer, etc.

3) **Dedication** - not all books need to contain a dedication page, but if they do it follows the copyright page.

4) **Epigraph** - this is typically a quote or an inspirational thought that is used to set the tone of the book and it can appear on its own page or on the backside of the Dedication page.

5) **Table of Contents (TOC)** - Fiction writers don't often include a TOC in a paperback version of their book, but Amazon requires a TOC in all Kindle versions. The style and contents of the TOC is often left up to the author.

6) **Foreword** - This is a short piece written by someone other than the author. It may be a page of praise for the content of the book and is signed by its writer. It is also referred to as a Blurb or page of praise.

7) **Preface** - This is written by the author and serves as a description of how the book came into being. It is often signed by the author.

Note: A more recent addition to e-book structure is the inclusion of the blurb (story description) in the location of the Foreword or the Preface. Some feel that this is a good point to refresh the reader's memory as to what the story line is. With readers taking advantage of books on sale, the books may languish on the reader's e-reader or e-reader app for some time before they are read. Not typically found in print books.

8) **Acknowledgments** - This section allows the author to recognize and express gratitude to contributors to the book.

9) **Introduction** - This section allows the author to ease the reader into the book by explaining the purpose and goals and may also explain the context of the book, how the content of the book is organized and perhaps the scope of the content.

10) **Prologue** - in Fiction, this section serves to set the scene for the story. It is told in the voice of a character, not the author's voice

B) **Body** serves as the main part of a book—the place where the chapters are.

1) **Chapter opening page** - also called the Chapter start page—typically is a right-hand page and the chapter identifier (number or name) is placed partway down the page with a small separation between that and the start of the text. If this book has section breaks or is divided into parts, each section or group will have an opening page that has a

number or title partway down the page. There would be no other body text on that type of page.

2) **Epilogue** - The epilogue is meant to be an ending section that brings closure to the story. It may be in the voice of the author or a continuation of the narrative.

3) **Afterword** - This section may be used to place the work into a wider context and is often written in the author's voice.

4) **Conclusion** - This section attempts to sum up the main points or arguments of the body of the work and bring it to a close.

C) **Back Matter** will contain a variety of notes, supporting material and information on the author and other books written by this author or related to the same subject matter. (Information about other books written by the author can also often be found in the front matter)

1) **Postscript** - Will serve as an addition or afterthought to the main part of the book

2) **Appendix** - Contains supplemental information to help the reader. More common in non-fiction and may contain source material or material that would detract from the narrative such as tables or lists of resource material

3) **Glossary** - An alphabetical list of terms and their definitions that are used in the book.

4) **Bibliography** - An ordered list of references used in the creation of the book. These books may or may not have been directly quoted from in the body of the book.

5) **List of Contributors** - Similar to the Acknowledgments section in the front mater, this section allows the author to name and thank people involved in the project. This section might literally be a list or it may be paragraphs of thanks.

6) **Index** - Only typically found in works of non-fiction and

is an alphabetical list of key words along with the associated page number where they can be found.

7) **Author bio** - It is common to include a brief bio and perhaps a picture of the author along with a list of various places the author can be found in the online world.

8) **Other books by or related books** - Authors typically include a brief outline of their other books and links to places they can be purchased. Sometimes excerpts from books are also found here. If the author chooses, they can promote other authors' books in this section—something that is commonplace with larger publishing houses. This information can be found in the front matter as well, but typically will be found in the back matter.

II

THE BASICS

5

ROADMAP/FLOWCHART

Now that we have the foundations covered, we should all be speaking the same language and be ready with some basic information to go forward and talk about the process of publishing a book in the modern era.

In this chapter we are going to talk about the big picture of publishing a book—the high level overview. And then in the following chapters, we'll cover details of each stop on the roadmap shown below:

Write a manuscript

Edit the manuscript

Get an ISBN from the appropriate source

Have a cover graphic created

Get the manuscript ready to be published

Where do I sell the book? (Or Where do I publish my book?)

Publish my book

Market the book

As you can see in the flowchart above, I see the process of publishing to be quite straightforward. Once a manuscript is finished (or almost finished), the next step is editing. The editing process is likely an extensive process involving your actions as well as the actions of professionals. If you like multitasking, you can apply for your ISBN while the editing process is taking place. If you aren't a multitasker, the step after editing is to get an ISBN. A cover graphic must also be created. When the editing process is finished, the manuscript and cover graphic are combined into a series of book files in preparation for uploading to a number of retail platforms. Once the upload process is finished, there is typically a verification process that takes a few hours to sometimes 48 hours depending on the platform. Once the verification process has been passed, the book will be live and available to be purchased in the retail locations chosen. I generally add a proofing step here, whether for the e-book, print or both, and I suggest both products be carefully scrutinized as this product is going to be sold to people to be read. The next job is to spread the word about this newly released book—marketing.

I'm sure you have many questions! What kind of editing do I need? Where do I find a good editor? What kind of files do I need? How do I create these files? And what the heck are the retailers?

In the following chapters of this book, we're going to cover all this information and more in a logical, no technobabble kind of way. I'm going to lead you through the steps involved, explain what each step entails and give you hints and tricks along the way. We'll talk about what retailers are, the information that is required at each step to walk confidently at each point. And I'll be providing you as many sources of information as I can find. Everything from writer's groups, to editors, to formatters, to places that report on the people who take advantage of authors...and sadly, there are too many of those. I'll back up everything I say with facts, figures and links to investigate by yourself.

That being said, let's move on to the first step in our roadmap—editing.

6

EDITING

M any writers assume that editing starts when the manuscript is complete. That isn't entirely true. Most writers will self-edit as they write. In my experience, writers set up a pattern, either starting each writing day by editing the previous day's work or something similar that fits their workflow. Many writers will take advantage of various bits and pieces of editing help during their journey to a finished product. They may sign up for a blue-pencil session at a conference, they may be part of a strong critique group that will guide their storyline development or in fact they may take advantage of a manuscript evaluation type of service to see if they are on the right track.

Everyone needs some form of editing! Even editors need editors. Many consider it the biggest mistake an indie author can make to believe they can edit their own work. Just as writers spend money on writing courses, seminars and conferences to make their writing better, editing should be just another part of that learning process. A trained, experienced editor is just as much of a teacher as a writing teacher. And most qualified editors have special skills that English teachers or writing teachers don't have.

A quick story. I was totally lost when I was trying to put together my first book. Let's face it, I'm a science grad. I'm really good at stating facts —listing observations in an experiment — but was lost going beyond that point. I had pages and pages of survey results. I had pages and pages of information about most of the material I felt should be included in the book I was trying to create. I didn't have a clue how to put everything together into a logical, readable how-to guide to help authors. A friend gave me the email address of a really good developmental editor and suggested I buy a few hours of this editor's time —see what I could learn. Learn I did. I was totally amazed at how much help I got in focusing my book from someone who hadn't even read what I'd written! I learned about framing the content, I learned about pacing, I learned about organizing my content into sections and chapters. Best money I've spent! What seemed like an insurmountable task was now achievable. Could I have gotten the same help if I had attempted to put the information together first? Absolutely. In fact once I was finished following my first set of instructions I went back to that same editor with my newly created manuscript. I learned some more —and did some rewriting.

As I said above, I believe that writers of all stripes can learn as much from editors as we can from writing teachers. I love the following quote:

Editors love words. They are a critical reader. If you hire an editor, they are your best reader: someone who will work with you to improve the message you are trying to convey.
(http://peavi.ca/hire-an-editor/what-do-editors-do/)

Let's move on and talk about the levels of editing that are available and what you can expect the fee to be.

Although editors can wear many hats in many industries, when we talk about the skills they bring to the world of editing novels, genre fiction or most non-fiction, we are generally talking about four specific levels or types of editing. These four are:

1) Developmental Editing

This level of editing can also be known as Substantive editing, Stylistic editing, Structural editing, Manuscript Appraisal/evaluation or Book Doctoring.

Developmental editing can be seen as the highest level of editing and the editor will look at the manuscript (which may or may not be finished) in a holistic fashion. A Developmental edit takes a deep look at a manuscript and will likely result in major rewrites. It involves clarifying the storyline (or if non-fiction, the presentation of the content) and possible reorganization of the project. There may be correction of spelling and grammar errors, but this type of editing focuses more on the big picture than the minutiae of the prose. Although this is the most expensive level of editing because of the work involved, it is where the most learning occurs. A developmental editor has special skills that many do not possess. They have the ability to "see" how much better the story would be if the timeline is reorganized, or if a part is plucked from the middle to become the beginning. And sadly, because of the work involved and potential final bill, it is often the level that is overlooked by many budget-conscious beginner authors.

2) Content Editing

This level of editing will examine overall structure and novel craft issues. It will look at logic of the story, plot, character arcs, believability, scene structure, tone, prose style, pacing, tension, opening hook, show/tell, dialogue, chapter endings and transitions (to quote from the website of my editor). This level of editing can be considered to be one step down from Developmental editing in terms of difficulty, complexity, and typically price and is often the starting point of most authors' foray into the world of editing.

Before we move on to Copy editing, I wanted to include information directly from an editor. I asked my editor to describe the difference between Developmental and Content editing and I loved her explanation so I'm including it below:

> "A developmental edit is a long process that can go on for a month to a year. Although both Developmental editing and Content editing address the basic elements of novel structure, or if nonfiction, the structure of a self-help or memoir or how to book, etc., the content edit gives the author a report and comments on what works in the book, what the problem issues are, and suggests what needs to be done with the manuscript—and that is it. Usually the editor is available for a minimal number of questions, but that is

all. The author goes off to complete the revisions on her own, and may or may not come back for a copy edit.

With a developmental edit, the content edit is only the first step. If the book is not yet written, then it would be a synopsis and outline that gets critiqued as a starting point. Then the editor works back and forth with the author, editing revised scenes or chapters as they are written, giving feedback on ideas for adjusting problem elements that just do not work.... In other words, the developmental edit can include a lot of handholding, and that is where the expensive price tag comes in."

3) Copy editing/line editing

This level of editing will look at grammar, spelling, punctuation and other mechanics of style. It will check for consistency of mechanics and internal consistency of facts. It may also include Canadianization (or making sure the language fits the source country or culture as desired).

4) Proofreading

This level of editing can be performed at several points on the journey to publishing. Often proofreading is done before the manuscript is formatted, but proofing can also be done on the "final" product. Reading through paper proof copies of a paperback book (usually called a galley) or an electronic version of an e-book is often considered to be the real final step before a book is available for sale to the public. Before formatting, it is often considered to be one last pass to catch any remaining typos, spacing or line issues and the like. Proofing of a paper proof copy of a book before it goes live to the public refers to all of the above, but also to looking at things like text placement on pages, location/clarity of any images or art, accuracy of page numbers, chapter starts, headers and footers.

According to Editors.ca an editor can expect to earn $60,000 a year in the industry on average. You should expect to pay a freelance editor about $60 an hour to edit your book. We're going to use this figure to do some calculations and find some benchmark pricing.

Sometimes the fee is calculated as an hourly rate; other times it is calculated as a flat project fee. Hourly rates vary depending on the type of work and the difficulty of the text. For example, a substantive edit of a document written by someone working with highly specialized language or by someone for whom English is a second language is more time-consuming than a proofread of a children's picture book.

Amy Einsohn's *The Copyeditor's Handbook*, Second Edition (University of California Press, 2006) provides the following guide for estimating the amount of time a particular project may take:

- Substantive, structural, or stylistic editing of a difficult text: 1 to 2 pages/hour
- Substantive, structural, or stylistic editing of a standard text: 2 to 3 pages/hour
  - Copy editing a difficult text: 2 to 4 pages/hour
  - Copy editing a standard text: 4 to 7 pages/hour
  - Proofreading a difficult text: 4 to 6 pages/hour
  - Proofreading a standard text: 6 to 9 pages/hour

Using these numbers and the assumption that one page contains 500 words as well as the assumption that a novel will contain 50,000 words, we can do some math.

A 50,000-word manuscript will be roughly 100 pages.

Assuming the 100 pages are relatively clean, a proofread would cost about $650.00. Using the same figures, a Substantive edit would be around $1000.00.

These numbers are meant to be a guide. In fact, freelance editors will set their own rates but you shouldn't expect them to be too far away from the norms. Editors are not all created equal, however. You should expect to pay for years of hard-won experience.

The question that always comes up is some version of "won't a retired English teacher or university English student do" for the job of editing? Most writers will tell you that editors have special skills that I see as a gift, not something that can be taught. English teachers or detail-oriented university students might be able to catch typos, but they likely won't bring needed skills to your project that could result in a much better end product.

Again, I turned to my editor and asked her for an explanation of her view of the difference between English teachers and editors. Again, I love her clarity, so I'm going to quote her:

"The main difference is that the book editor has to know the publishing marketplace, and it has different rules and requirements than a term paper and different goals than classic literature. A book editor has to know genre-specific requirements and what kind of language and story structure are expected in each. An English teacher focuses on literature as an art form and its place in cultural history rather than as a commercial product, but once you get into the selling of books, even current literary fiction, the editor and publisher have to focus on how it fits in the marketplace and what appeals to the target readers."

Love this quote—I hope it does a great job of convincing you to hire a great editor.

"Editing is one of the absolute factors that will influence your book sales. The degree to which you personally edit your thoughts and writing, combined with the degree to which you invest in professional editing will ultimately play a large role in developing reader comfort. A great edit will not ensure your book sells, but it will definitely eliminate one of the largest potential detractors that might prevent book sales."
~Lulu blog

As the quote above suggests, it is very likely that the money you pay for an editor will be returned to you many times over in terms of sales of your book.

Where to find an editor

I am the area representative of the Federation of BC Writers—a Canadian provincially focused resource group for authors. A question I often field is about how to find a qualified editor.

Editors don't need to live locally to you and don't even have to live in the same country as you. Communication with an editor is not an "in person" event. It involves emailing a Word document and having it returned to you with either a separate document of comments/change suggestions and/or the original Word doc with Track Changes enabled and comments/changes attached to words or phrases.

I feel that the geographical distance actually helps relationships with editors. I recently had a writer insist that she wanted an editor that she could meet with in person so that she could guide the editor through her thought process for the project. I pointed out that the editor needed to be unbiased—to come at the project without preconceived ideas. An editor worthy of their pile of red pens and years of experience wouldn't need an explanation from the writer to make a book better. Keep in mind that an editor doesn't rewrite a book, they may actually change glaring grammar and spelling errors, but they will make suggestions to the writer in writing on how to improve the storyline or help with plot inconsistencies. The writer has the ability to dismiss the suggestions of an editor, but a writer that goes into the editing process looking to learn and having chosen well, likely won't face that situation.

Getting back to the question of where to find an editor. The most accomplished editors are well known within the industry and many of the best are no longer taking new clients. For the beginner author who has few contacts in the industry, finding a qualified person can be a struggle.

For those in this situation, I suggest starting with national or provincial associations of editors. I've listed several in the Appendix of this book. These associations will allow their members to create profiles that are often searchable by keyword. You will want to find an editor that is familiar with your genre and comfortable with the level of editing you are interested in. For example, if you write Young Adult Fantasy, you will want someone who is familiar with the genre and current with trends in the industry.

Search through the listings for two or three editors who sound like they would be a good fit for your project. Make contact (they should have an email contact point) with a note describing your project with details on the size of your manuscript, your genre and most importantly, your deadline. Editors can be booked quite some time in advance! Generally speaking, editors will get back to you within a few days and you can have an email discussion about your project. Editors will know what questions they want answered from you and should be willing to provide references and proof of competency. In fact many will offer to do a sample edit of a few pages or a chapter to see if you can work with their style. The list that I've included can serve as a starting point - it is not an exhaustive list, but don't be afraid to search Google for an association specific to the country you live in.

Editors' rates can vary depending on the project, but ultimately they work on a fee-for-service basis. They will provide an assessment and an estimate of the final charge. Many will require a written agreement, either in the form of a letter or a formal contract that clearly specifies the scope of the work and the fees either as an hourly rate or as a fixed price for the project.

Since life can occasionally interfere, there should be open communication between the writer and the editor so that the writer can be apprised of delays or difficulties found and vice versa.

As I'll mention several times in this book, writers are often the target of an excellent sales job. The offers of a "Manuscript evaluation" or "Book Doctoring" are often a way of separating a writer from their money. Many shady self-publishing services will offer an evaluation to determine if the book will be "accepted," when in fact they accept every book because the author pays for all the services. We'll talk about "self-publishing services" in a future chapter. Many beginner authors are quite intimidated by the process of publishing their own book and they choose to use a service—many of which are a bit shady, or in some cases, completely lacking in ethics. I bring this up here as one service that these companies usually offer is some level of editing. I like the quote that I pulled from a book that the Alliance of Independent Authors created entitled: *Choosing a Self-Publishing Company*:

> *"Be wary of a provider that will not give the name of a specific publishing professional or the name of an affiliate service it uses.*
>
> *A good service will always advise you on what work is required to improve your book. You should also be free to work with any other external service or professional you wish in conjunction with your chosen service.*
>
> *Never accept the line, "Oh, we only accept books using our editing/design services." If the provider cannot be flexible, then take your business elsewhere."*
>
> *~ ALLi*

The homework that I'm going to assign for the end of this chapter is to start your search for a writer's group to join. I'm a huge fan of networking. Writing doesn't need to be, nor should it be a solitary occupation. And the journey to publishing is a journey that is filled with other people— from other supportive writers to skilled people that can help with tasks that you aren't comfortable doing yourself. Editing is a great example of one of those tasks.

In the previous section we talked about where to find an editor. There are local and national organizations of editors that can serve as one starting point, but other authors and writer's organizations can help as well.

Back to the idea of finding a writer's group...I'd like you to find a writer's group that suits your needs. I've supplied an extensive, but I'm sure not an exhaustive list in the Appendix of this book. In Canada, writer's groups can be divided into four types (and I've listed examples from my local area):

1. National – for example Canadian Authors which I'm a member of

2. Provincial/State/County – for example Federation of BC Writers for which I'm an area representative

3. Local – for example Golden Ears Writers in Maple Ridge, BC

4. Genre specific – for example Sisters in Crime or Romance Writers of America

Depending on where you live, look locally, look regionally, look nationally for writer's groups. You will find them!

There are different reasons for joining different groups. Most groups in Canada are funded by grant money and can be great sources of information. As we will talk about in this book, Self-Publishing can be a challenging endeavor. Finding people who know what they are doing is one of the more challenging aspects. Writer's groups have lists of contacts—even lists on their websites sometimes—and they have other writers who know someone who can help. Getting out and talking with other writers can solve problems and can even help you find the best editor in the world for you!

7

I S B N S

The next stop on our roadmap is to apply for an ISBN. To start out this chapter, let's define and describe an ISBN for those who are not familiar.

An ISBN (International Standard Book Number) is a 13-digit number that uniquely identifies each specific edition of a book or book-like product (an example of a book-like product can be an e-book). If you are interested in the details of what the sets of numbers involved in an ISBN mean, I've included a full definition in the Glossary at the back of this book.

In practicalities, what's an ISBN? It is simply a unique identifying feature. Every ISBN is different. Going back to the example from your first piece of homework and if you remember, the ISBN was found on the back of the book as part of the bar code. It should also be found on the copyright page.

An ISBN is issued for a publication where text stands on its own as a product, whether in print, audio or electronic format. Of the list of items that qualify for ISBNs, the ones that may apply to writers are:

- Audiobooks
- Books
- Brochures
- E-books (digital books)
- Graphic novels
- Picture books
- Story books

Interestingly, coloring books do not need an ISBN.

The next question I often field is "Why should I bother getting an ISBN when I can easily get one from Amazon?" Granted, I often field this question from the authors I work with who have to pay for ISBNs, but I also get this question from Canadian authors who can receive ISBNs for free from their government. The quick answer is that you want to be shown as the author/publisher of record. I don't care if you decide to set up a small publishing umbrella to publish your own books or if you use your own name as the publisher, if you don't use your own ISBNs, Amazon, Kobo, etc. will show as the publisher of record of your books. What this means is if a bookstore is looking to purchase copies of your book, Amazon likely shows as the publisher of record. This is a glaring way of letting everyone know that your book is self-published. The average reading public won't understand. The average reader doesn't check out who the publisher is before purchasing a book, but bookstores understand. The next question would be: "Are bookstores easily fooled by a one-off publishing name?" Probably not. However, some of the overt stigma is removed.

Here is your next piece of homework. Go into your local

bookstore and ask from where they order their books. Unless the bookstore that you walked into is an Independent bookstore (NOT Chapters or Barnes & Noble for example), they likely have procedures set in stone from their head office. And likely they wouldn't order books from Amazon even if they could. Various reasons for that that we'll talk about in a future chapter, but for now, go and ask some questions. Find out some information and we'll come back to this.

How to get an ISBN

Where you get your ISBN will depend on the country you live in. Most countries will have a dedicated granting institution - in many cases as a division of the government but some are private companies. For an overall search guide, the International ISBN Agency (https://www.isbn-international.org) provides a starting place to search for most countries.

Let's talk about the major names in the ISBN world.

Bowker is the official ISBN Agency for the US and its territories and Australia (although in Australia the company name is Thorpe-Bowker). Their website can be found http://www.bowker.com/. The quote from its website states:

"Bowker is the world's leading provider of bibliographic information and management solutions designed to help publishers, authors, and booksellers better serve their customers. Creators of products and services that make books easier for people to discover, evaluate, order, and experience. Bowker is the official ISBN Agency for the United States and its territories and Australia. A ProQuest affiliate, Bowker is headquartered in New Providence, New Jersey with additional operations in the United Kingdom and Australia."

Note: One item that is often offered for purchase is a barcode that matches your ISBN. If you are publishing via KDP Print or IngramSpark, they supply the barcode as part of the printing process. (or in the case of IngramSpark, the barcode is supplied as part of the cover template) There is no need to purchase one or have your graphic designer create one for your book cover.

Bowker is very organized and provides quite a bit of assistance. I've included a link to a PDF they offer which many new authors find very helpful. Like most of the ISBN sites, your first step is to create a free account and purchase the number of ISBNs you need. Keep in mind that you will need one ISBN for each format of your book. For example if you wish to sell a paperback, e-book and audiobook version, you will need 3 ISBNs.

Logging into your free account after purchasing the ISBNs, you will be allowed to assign those numbers by filling in title details in the fields provided. Complete details can be followed in the PDF that Bowker provides.

Nielson is the official ISBN Agency for the UK and Ireland. They can be found http://www.isbn.nielsenbook.co.uk A great introduction to their services can be found on a helpful PDF they provide:

http://www.isbn.nielsenbook.co.uk/uploads/Independe nt%20Publisher%20Brochure%202017_Digital(2).pdf

I like the opening quote from the Nielson PDF:

"Whether you're contemplating writing your own book or publishing titles for other authors, we can help you understand the book supply chain. We can guide you through the process from purchasing ISBNs to receiving orders online, enhancing your book metadata and using book widgets to ensure you reach the widest possible audience and sell more copies of your books. We can also help you understand the market and show you how your titles and those of your competitors are selling."

The point of purchase for ISBNs for Nielson is: https://www.nielsenisbnstore.com/. With Nielson, like with Bowker, the process to obtain ISBNs is quite straight-forward. The author opens a free account and purchases the appropriate number of ISBNs. Information is then entered about the book and saved. What I found interesting is authors can submit their ISBNs to Nielson for inclusion on their database for free.

As a final note, please make sure that you use the International ISBN Agency site and search for the appro-priate information for the country you live in. One of the biggest mistakes I made early on was to purchase a block of

ISBNs from Bowker. I was following reference material from American sources and was completely unaware at that time that Canadians (like me) were provided ISBNs for free. That was $250.00US that I didn't need to spend and I'll never get back. Canada is not the only country who provides free ISBNs to its citizens.

Legal Deposit

The last subject to add to this chapter is that of Legal Deposit. Almost every country requires authors/publisher deposit a copy (or 2 copies) of their book once it has been published (either paperback, audiobook or e-book). A quick Google search will provide you with the appropriate source of information for your country as well as the details required for this submission. You will also be provided with some guidance from the ISBN granting agency that you use.

We will now move on to the topic of cover graphics - the next step in the flowchart or roadmap.

8

COVER GRAPHIC

The next step in our roadmap is the creation of a cover graphic for your book. Choosing the perfect cover graphic for my books has always been my greatest problem point.

What will grab readers' attention in a thumbnail size? What is and where can a thumbnail-sized cover graphic be found? What best fits with the genre of the book? So many questions.

In this chapter we are going to talk about the specifics of what a cover graphic is, how to figure out what the requirements are, and lastly we're going to talk about some places to start a search for a cover graphic artist.

Before moving into the material for this chapter, I'm going to strongly suggest that you don't try to make the cover graphic for your first book by yourself. Even if you have some graphic skills, or have a photo or graphic that you want to have on the front cover of your book, consider working with an experienced person in a partnership situation. From determining what size is needed for each cover, to choosing fonts, to calculating the spine width for a paperback cover to what format the file needs to be in, an experienced partner goes a long way. As the saying goes: "First impressions count" and "We judge a book by its cover." You need to get your cover graphic right and a professional can provide guidance. I believe a professional is well worth the money.

Let's start with the first section of this chapter—the specifics of what a cover graphic is. To help you understand what needs to be created, I'm going to assign you three exercises.

Three homework assignments:

1) Log onto your computer—or better yet grab your smart phone or tablet—and go to Amazon.com or Amazon.ca or whatever your local Amazon site is and do some window-shopping. Search for and find some of your favorite books. Look at what the cover graphics look like in the search screen—what we call "thumbnails" lined up on your screen. The word "thumbnail" is used to refer to a small-sized version of a graphic. Click on an entry and you'll see a slightly larger cover graphic along with the details of the book. To point out the obvious, a cover graphic on a retail site is much smaller than the cover of a paperback book that you can hold in your hands.

2) Pick up that paperback book that we've been referring to throughout this book. Look at the cover that is on that book. Spread the book out so that you can look at the front and back cover at once. This graphic is different than the one above—it is bigger; it has a spine; it has writing (and maybe a graphic) on the back as well as the front.

3) For extra homework points go to your favorite bookstore and wander the aisles looking at books. You'll notice that some of the books will be face out and some will be spine out on the shelves. Other books will be arranged in

different types of displays on tables or at the end of shelves resulting in more of the book being visible.

Let's talk about what you found. The first and obvious point is that you will create (or will have a book designer create) two types of cover graphics—one for an electronic book and another for a paperback book. The graphic for the electronic book will be displayed in the online retailers. Regardless of whether a reader is looking at the record for an e-book version or a paperback version of the book, they will see the simple rectangle of an e-book cover. This is a really important point! The cover created for a paperback book is only viewed in its entirety when the paperback is in someone's hands. Some retailers will show two graphics when viewing the paperback record online—one for the front and one for the back. However, the graphics for a paperback book—the front cover, the spine and the back cover—are never viewed by readers online as one unit.

The reason that I say this is very important is because we are going to differentiate between content that is visible and readable for the front cover graphic and content that you place on the back cover that never really needs to be read on a tiny screen.

The next thing that you likely noticed in the first assignment is the thumbnail cover graphics that can be seen on Amazon and other online retailers are pretty small. It is often difficult to read all the text on a cover. We'll expand on this further on in this chapter.

Let's move on to what else you found in your explorations. You should have noticed that the e-book graphic is a rectangle, in what's called portrait orientation, in other words, it is taller than it is wide. A paperback graphic is also a rectangle, but it is wider than it is tall. A paperback graphic can be divided into three sections: the front graphic, the spine, and the back graphic/matter.

You may have found a paperback book that had a graphical element that spanned the front and back of the cover. You many have found some paperback books that have a distinct graphic on the front cover, but the back cover was just a similar color to the front or a texture that carried over from the front. Hopefully you noticed the readability of the text on the back cover as well as what exactly is on the back cover of a book. Was there a picture of the author? Was there a brief bio of the author? Was there an endorsement from a well-known author? We'll talk about all these further on.

When you wandered through the bookstore, did you notice how little of the book was visible? Many books only have their spine showing. If the cover graphics are being used to sell the book, or as part of the sales mechanisms of the book, how is that possible when only the spine shows?

Now that we have moved this far in our learning, I'm going to give you another piece of homework. I want you to go to Amazon.com or Amazon.ca or whatever your local Amazon site is and look at books in your genre. I want you to look at books in the genre in which you wish to sell yours.

Note: I work with authors all the time that feel their book is unique, that it can't be tied down to one genre. That may be true; however, part of publishing a book is to assign it to a category—a genre. You will actually be allowed to attach it to several categories, but regardless, you will need to choose a genre. Perhaps this exercise will help you in this journey.

The books in your genre will have a similar look and feel. Just like wandering the aisles at a bookstore and finding a cover that speaks to you, the cover graphic will, among other things, help the reader understand the genre. To generalize, Horror is dark and scary, Romance shows a couple embracing, Erotic Romance shows body parts and is suggestive, and SciFi shows otherworldly beings/graphics.

The font that is used for the title of the book should be readable in thumbnail size—which is sometimes difficult to do. Although a clear and crisp serif font is easier to read, it perhaps doesn't fit with the genre. As an example, Historical Romance covers tend to have a script font for the title, while the same is not true for a Thriller cover. And as I suggested, you want to fit within your genre.

Let's go back to the exercise where you looked at the other books in your genre on Amazon. Readers use cover graphics to make a buying decision —perhaps not just using the cover alone, but it will be part of the puzzle — and they also use the cover to place the book in the appropriate genre. For example, I would never buy a Historical Romance that had things being blown up, or bloody bodies on the front cover. To me, that type of graphic would place the book in the Thriller category and I would dismiss it as a possible book of interest to me.

We want the cover graphic to speak to the story in some fashion. Let's take an example of a Historical Fiction book. The graphic should speak to the storyline as well as the period the story is placed in. If a story is set in London, England, in medieval times, it shouldn't have the Statue of Liberty in the graphic.

You are probably saying to yourself that you want your cover to stand out, to be different. You do and you don't. You want a cover graphic that will fit in the genre, yet be eye-catching and unique to attract interested readers—but at the same time, be understandable or readable at the thumbnail size.

Are you starting to understand why you would want the guidance of a professional for at least the creation of your first cover graphic? It is advisable to have experienced help to make an informed decision about this important selling point for your book.

Useful Definitions and Dimensions

There are many ways to achieve a cover graphic for your book, and we'll discuss some starting points below. If you are hiring a designer, there are two basic levels of starting points.

- **Premade covers** are graphics that designers put together for a quick sale. Generally speaking, the designer just adds your name and the title of your book and the graphic is ready for your use.

- **Custom covers or custom designs** tend to take longer and are usually more expensive. These graphics are put together from scratch. The designer will ask some questions and often present several choices for you to pick from.

Either type of cover can be created from original art or stock photos (photos bought from services that sell them such as Shutterstock or iStockPhoto). There is usually a significant difference in price between the two.

Let's move on to the actual dimensions and specifications of a cover graphic. The graphic that you will either create or obtain from your graphic designer will be really big. The minimum size that is recommended is 1600 pixels X 2400 pixels. But first the basic requirements.

E-book cover

Height/width ratio of 1:1.6 (for Amazon/KDP) or 1:1.5 (for most other retailers)

File type - jpeg/jpg or tif/tiff

Required size - 1600px X 2560px (for Amazon) or 1600 X 2400 (for all other retailers)

File Size & resolution - must be less than 50MB and a resolution of 72dpi

Color - products display on the website using RGB color mode (do not use CMYK or sRBG)

Borders - cover art with a white background or very light backgrounds seem to disappear against the white background of many retail sites - consider adding a narrow border to define the edges of the cover graphic

Paperback cover

Height/width are determined according to a number of factors. Print on Demand retailers such as KDP Print and IngramSpark have templates that can be downloaded to help with sizing. (https://kdp.amazon.com/en_US/cover-templates)

File type - PDF only

Content - the title, subtitle, author name and series information on the cover must match the information entered in the book record and must be legible. KDP Print will kick out covers that contain a mismatch between cover content and book details.

Spine text can only be used if the paperback has a minimum of 100 pages

Resolution - the finished product must have a minimum resolution of 300 dpi. Even if the graphic used to create the PDF has multiple layers, it will all be flattened to one layer. For more information on multiple layer graphics and resolution, see the appendix.

Resources that will help with cover creation

Although I've shared my personal opinion on hiring a professional for your cover, there are do-it-yourself sites or low-cost sites that can be used.

Quote from Smashwords:

> *"Things to look for when you hire a professional: Ask if they'll provide both print and e-book covers and how many revisions you will be able to make. Also, if possible, you want to keep the raw files. That way, if you have changes later, you won't have to have someone start from scratch — they can simply edit minor things (which will save you money). Make sure they will design the cover according to your printer's specs, which can vary."*

Do it yourself

KDP has a program called "Cover Creator" that you can use to put a cover together for your e-book and paperback respectively. This is a free resource. See the appendix for a link to this service.

Pressbooks.com also has a cover generator that comes free with their upper level plan purchase.

Canva.com is a free/paid website that allows for easy creation of many different types of graphics. I don't believe that it will allow for the creation of a paperback book cover, but it has a template for an e-book cover. Many of the functions of Canva are free, but it is possible to spend money on graphics, fancy fonts and sample layouts.

Services

Fiverr.com is an online marketplace where you can

purchase services for $5.00 and up (hence the name). Feel free to wander through the offerings and see what can be had for what price.

99 designs (https://99designs.ca/pricing) This company will have you fill out a profile of what you are looking for, choose a package, and designers will compete for your project by creating suggestions. As of this writing, the packages start at $389US.

In addition to these suggestions, there are a variety of other places where you can look for graphic designers. Many larger writing groups have members that are graphic designers who can serve as a starting point in your search. Unlike editors or professional writers, there isn't a national organization of graphic designers, especially ones that deal with book cover graphics.

For a list of other designers, including people who have helped me with book covers, please see the list in the Appendix.

In the next chapter we are going to talk about getting your manuscript ready to be published.

III

GETTING THE MANUSCRIPT READY FOR PUBLISHING

9

GET THE MANUSCRIPT READY

In this section we are going to talk about the steps that are required to get a book ready to be published. Some of this information is a bit technical, but I feel that it is necessary to cover this material. In my experience, this is the point where authors tend to stumble. This is where they get lost in the terms used—more words that aren't used in normal conversation.

The steps that we will talk about in this section are often what is referred to as Formatting. The definition of formatting that we are going to use here is:

"To convert a manuscript into the various files that are needed for publishing."

Formatting can also be called Manuscript Conversion, Typesetting, Layout or Book Designing.

The term that many writers are most familiar with is Typesetting. If we look at the dictionary, typesetting is defined as: *"the process of setting material in type or into a form to be used in printing."* If we go back in history, in order to **print** a book, the letters and words had to be organized in a frame in order to be reproduced on paper. We had to "set the type."

Most modern printing is digital and no longer involves the manual process of setting type in a frame; however, the term has carried on. Today's process of printing and publishing involves changing the format of files into a type or style required.

Many writers finish the writing and editing process with a Word document or equivalent. We are going to start our discussion with this humble Word document. Regardless of what format you create your manuscript in, you will likely end up with a Word document to send to your editor. And before you ask, yes, there are editors that will take a variety of types of documents from Apple Pages to open source documents, but Microsoft Word is the industry standard. Likely the majority of you will be writing on and manipulating this program.

As was mentioned above, having a clean manuscript file is one of the struggles authors face. We type, delete and move around content. Our editors markup the document adding their thoughts. All of these actions can introduce weird things into our Word document. I'm sure you've seen it—spaces that just won't go away, odd sentence fragments that look lonely at the end of a page and so on.

Let's start this section with a list of tips and tricks:

1) Do not use the tab key or space bar to create paragraph indents—use the formatting options in Word to set the first line of every paragraph to indent.

2) Do not include page numbers in a manuscript that is going to be converted to an electronic book. As we found out when playing with various e-readers, page numbers are not used in electronic books, locations and percentages read are—page number can create some issues.

3) Apply a "heading 1" style to all chapter heads/titles so that they can easily be identified as different than other text.

4) Insert a page break at the end of every chapter to ensure that a chapter start is identified properly and to ensure that the new chapter starts on a new "page."

5) Fancy fonts (especially fancy serif fonts) can be changed into strange characters and/symbols resulting in what I would refer to as artifacts, but others describe as a "garbled mess." Ensure that the body text and title texts are in a common font like Times or Geneva.

6) If you have bold or italic font or underlining, format the font from the menu or the buttons on the tool bar of Word.

7) Don't use accent symbols like Wingdings, symbols or special characters that are not on the keyboard in a manuscript that will be formatted into an electronic book. These types of characters often don't format well.

8) The process involved in getting a file ready to publish will go smoother if you choose font size that is close to normal. Choose a 10 or 12- point font for the body text and 14 or 18 point for chapter titles. Any font that is very small or very large will likely cause formatting issues.

9) Images can cause issues. To avoid potential problems, center images, don't have the text wrap around, include a description (alt text) as part of your picture so that something shows if the picture can't be displayed, and make sure your pictures are .jpg or .png. Images in e-books only need to be 72dpi but need to be 300 dpi in paper books.

10) Try to avoid tables unless inserted as jpgs. Tables don't often behave well in electronic books.

The next subject we will talk about is the file types involved in the process of publishing. Sometimes seen as a technical subject, but a necessary one to help cut through confusion.

10

FILE FORMATS

In the previous chapter we talked about some tips and tricks to creating a clean Word document. In this chapter we're going to talk more about Word as well as about the three other file types for the process of "publishing."

As we'll see in future chapters, the process of modern publishing is simply the upload of a file to a website. The composition and structure of that file can take a number of forms. If you think back to your homework exercise with an e-reader or e-reader app, you'll realize that we need to create a product that looks good on a small screen as well as creating a product that looks good in paperback form.

You'll hear me comment several times through this book that I'm pretty fussy about how my books look in all forms. I make specific choices for specific reasons. But as I commented in the first chapter of this book, there are many choices available when it comes to publishing and this section will illustrate some of the choices that are available.

Ultimately, it is possible to publish a book using only a well-structured Word document, but there are other choices also. To understand those choices, we need to go through an explanation of the four file types that can be used in publishing a book. Once you have a handle on the new words you will be adding to your vocabulary, we will talk about various methods available to create these types of files.

The four file types that we are going to talk about in this chapter are:

- DOC/DOCX files
- PDF files
- MOBI files
- EPUB files

1) **A DOC or DOCX** file is likely familiar to you. These are the file types used by Microsoft Word. As an aside here, the author/publishing world tends to revolve around Microsoft Word. Many of us complain, in fact regularly curse at our Word documents, but they are a standard tool in the writing world. I am aware that there are many other word processing programs available for use, but Word is the industry standard. Will you be able to find an editor who will edit on a Pages document or an Open Office document? Likely, as many editors are quite technical.

> **Note:** As will be discussed below, Word is the gold standard file format and serves as the basis of all other file types we will use. Even if you can submit a Macintosh

Pages document to an editor, you will likely need to convert it to a .doc or .docx file for formatting.

Let's define this file type. A quick search of Microsoft's documents tells me that a DOC or DOCX file (or .doc or .docx) are Microsoft Word document files. If you have an older version of Word, it likely saves in DOC (or .doc) and if that file is opened in a Word program from after 2007, it will open in "Compatibility Mode" and will prefer to save in DOCX (.docx)

If you look at the title of your Manuscript file on your computer it will be written as "MyManuscriptTitle.doc" or "MyManuscriptTitle.docx"

One point you should keep in mind and that may be the source of much cursing as you ~~try to wrestle your Word doc to the floor and make it do what you want~~ format it, is that the text of a Word document has style coding that comes with it. It has paragraphs, indents, bold or italicized letter/words and so on. When we move the text from a Word document it will bring with it the associated style information. This is a good thing or a bad thing, depending on what you are trying to do.

2) Let's move on to the next file type on our list — **a PDF (Portable Document Format) file**. The PDF file type was originally created by Adobe and at the time only viewed on Adobe software. Many programs can now open and view a PDF file and, in fact, many programs can create a PDF file type.

PDF text is static. Try this experiment: Open a PDF document on a phone or tablet screen—something smaller than a desktop or laptop-sized screen. Since the text is static, if there are 400 words on a PDF page when you create it, there will still be 400 words on the page viewed on a phone or tablet screen. Those 400 words may be too small to read, unless you enlarge the page with your fingers and then move it around with your finger in order to read everything on the page.

I want you to think about your experiments with e-readers and apps. Remember I asked you to play with font size and line spacing? The text on an e-reader is fluid, not static. Clearly, a PDF isn't the best file format for an e-reader! As we'll talk about shortly, it is an allowable file type for uploading to several retailers, but in my experience, it doesn't always produce the nicest-looking e-book.

It is the gold-standard file type for creating a print book, however. Since the text is static (or often people use the term frozen) what you see on a PDF document is exactly what you will see on the pages of a book. There are many different ways to create a PDF file, and they aren't all created equal. We'll talk about those shortly.

3) Let's move on to the third file type on the list from above: **MOBI.** Mobi (.mobi) is short for Mobipocket. This is the file type that Amazon requires. Amazon bases its AZM file format on mobi. Kindle devices and apps support mobi files. A mobi (.mobi) file is meant for plain text or e-books with very few graphical elements. It puts a very low cap on image size, and as a result, images and graphics suffer in this file type.

One thing you discovered, hopefully, when playing with a Kindle device or Kindle app is that the focus for an e-reader is on text. When you fuss with settings, you are allowed to change the font family, font size, line justification and line separation. There isn't any setting for size of images, or placement of images. In reality, the e-reader is aimed at reading books, not viewing pictures. E-readers excel for genre fiction, but not for picture books.

That being said, Amazon is always trying to move toward their view of the future. A recent addition to their technologies is what's called Kindle in Motion. I stumbled on a Kindle in Motion book one night by accident and ended up using it as a demonstration in a workshop the next day. This type of Kindle book can't be viewed on a plain Kindle, but it can be viewed on an App on a computer or tablet, or some of the more advanced Kindle devices. Do a search on Amazon for Kindle in Motion, buy one of the choices and see what Amazon thinks the future holds! E-books in Amazon's Kindle in Motion books have little gifs or moving pictures.

4) The last file type from above is an **ePub**. This type of file is considered a standard file format for e-reader devices and e-reader applications (or Apps) other than those from Amazon. It is the most widely adopted e-book format. In terms of structure, an ePub file is more closely related to web pages than it is text documents. An ePub file contains various coding files and can even contain multimedia files. Of all the formats it is the most flexible, and because of this, it is the file type that is most often used for e-book files with detailed illustrations. Even with all that being said, Amazon does not use ePub files for its Kindle books.

Let's move on to the architecture of a book—the parts and pieces that make up a book.

11

STRUCTURE DETAILS OF
A BOOK

Regardless of the genre of your book, there are a variety of structural details (some refer to these as style details) that need to be present to follow formatting convention. Some of these details apply only to paperback books and others apply to paperback as well as e-books.

Before we dive into this content, pick up that handy paperback and have a quick look. You'll realize that the book is a specific size, the text on the pages is set back from the edges of the page and there is likely common content at the top and bottom of the pages. Let's do the same for an electronic book—there are commonalities as well as differences. The text will fill whatever the screen size is, but it will be set back from the edges. There aren't page numbers but location references or percentage read numbers. There may or may not be information above the body text of the book.

With all that information fresh in your mind, I'm going to add more new words to your vocabulary, and explain not only what some of the structural details of a book are, but also where they do and do not apply.

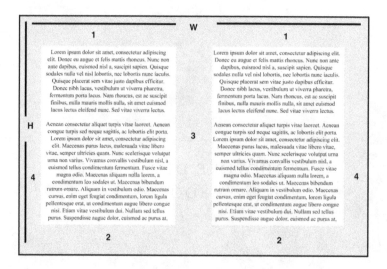

Diagram of Paperback page layout

H x W = Trim Size

1 - Header space

2 - Footer space

3 - Inside Margin or Gutter

4 - Outside Margin

1) Trim Size - This refers to the finished size of a paperback book expressed in inches. It does not apply to e-books. A typical size for a genre fiction book is 51/2 X 81/2 inches (width X height) and a typical size for a non-fiction is 6 X 9 inches. Although there are common trim sizes, I suggest that you measure books in your house or visit a bookstore and measure a few books in your genre. You want your book to fit in with its peers. Although this is not as important for books bought and sold online, as they aren't displayed for sale on a bookshelf, it is really important for books you want sold in physical bookstores. You want the books to look uniform on a bookshelf, and in fact, you want the book to actually fit on the shelf display.

Most Print on Demand services offer a variety of trim sizes. I have a list in the Appendix for your reference.

One key point that I'll throw in here is that as an Indie author we are offered a limited choice of trim sizes at the two main Print on Demand companies. That may feel confining for those of you who want to express your creativity in a unique book trim size.

Let's go back to the idea that a genre fiction or non-fiction book needs to fit norms. Not only for shelf space in a bookstore or in someone's home, you also will want your book to belong or fit in.

2) Margins - Margins refers to the spaces that are found around the text area for each page. These spaces are top and bottom as well as on each side. As we did previously, grab a paperback book and flip through some of the pages.

The first thing that you'll notice in a paperback book is the space in the middle when the book is open. What is called the "gutter" is space that exists on the right-hand page and left-hand page. That space is also referred to as the inside margin and will need to be large enough to allow for comfortable reading. If text is printed too far into the gutter, the reader may have to break the spine of the book in order to read it. We don't want this happening! Typically the gutter or inside margin is larger in size than the outside margin size.

Likewise the outside margins—the space between the end of the line of text and the edge of the page—need to allow for the placement of fingers holding the book without covering up letters.

The top and bottom margins—also referred to as the header and the footer—need to allow enough room for the header text to be placed and perhaps the page numbers to appear in the footer.

A common mistake on many self-published books is making the margins too small. Many self-publishers choose to use the minimum sizes given by KDP Print, IngramSpark or other Print on Demand service providers. I think that many authors don't realize that the numbers given are minimums.

In fact, one of the hallmarks of a traditionally published book is said to be an open, airy feel to the text. At a conference I was at recently, I overheard an agent telling an author that he could tell a self-published book from a traditionally published book by just glancing through the pages. He went on to say that self-published books look too cramped because the authors are trying to save money.

Let's address this comment. Most Print on Demand services such as KDP Print and IngramSpark have a guide to help authors price their book. They will state the break-even point—the price required to print and cover the selling fees. Any price an author chooses above that point is what they will make on each sale. The price of producing a book is based on a number of factors that we'll discuss in more detail in a future chapter, but the fewer the pages a book has, the lower the break-even price. It is not unusual for authors to use narrow margins, smaller font size and a variety of other means to reduce the number of pages and keep the cost down to the reader.

Going back to sizing the margins, the margin size, especially the inside margin or gutter, will depend on the number of pages in a book. The more pages you have, the larger this measurement should be.

A quote from Joel Friedlander, the Book Designer (https://www.thebookdesigner.com/)

"...so we know the gutter (or inside) margin on bound books has to be larger than the outer margin, but how much? Let's take a 6" x 9" book as an example. For a typical novel or narrative nonfiction book of about 200 pages, I would start off with an outside margin of .75" and a gutter margin of .875".

Remember that because our margins aren't even, our pages are asymmetrical, although if you look at your book as a series of two-page spreads, the whole layout is neatly and symmetrically arranged around the spine at the center."

As you can see from Joel's quote, when trying to figure out margin sizes, we picture the book being displayed as a 2-page display to mimic what a paper book looks like when open. You'll notice the numbers that he throws into this quote. All the Print on Demand vendors have guidelines. I've included a few samples in the References section at the back of this book. To use KDP Print as an example, they suggest an outside margin of .25 inches and a gutter of .375 for a 200-page book. Compare those numbers to what Joel is suggesting, and I would suggest being closer to Joel's numbers than the minimums given by KDP Print. Make your book comfortable to read.

Going back to the comment about price. Readers will choose to buy your book based on the content and the description. Scrimping on margins to save your readers a few pennies won't change a buying decision.

3) Headers and Footers - Although the Header and Footer space is often considered a margin, I'm going to talk about these areas separately. Let's take another quick peek at that paperback I've asked you to reference. You'll notice there is likely text and numbers in the spaces created at the top and bottom of the pages. As the names of the spaces suggests, we call the text/numbers at the top header text and we call the text/numbers at the bottom of the pages footer text.

Most books—be they fiction or non-fiction—have header text and sometimes page numbers. The text is usually the author's name on one facing page and the title of the book on the other facing page. Sometimes it is the title of the book and the name of the chapter on either page. Pages are numbered either at the top in the header or at the bottom in the footer. If you look at a collection of books, you'll likely see a variety of displays and combinations. Sometimes the page numbers are in the header at the outside page edge, sometimes in the footer centered on the page. From my research, I don't believe there is a style that is more correct than another. Let's view this as a preference. You choose what you want to display and in this section, we're going to talk about creating enough space for whatever you choose to display comfortably.

According to most guidelines, if you are creating a 6X9-inch trim size book, you will end up with 30 to 35 lines of text on the pages of your book. The variation in the number of lines will depend on the size and type of the font. This will easily allow for a header space of about .75 inches and a footer of .5 inches. And this space should comfortably allow for text to be displayed in the header and even allow for page numbers in the footers.

4) Font type and size - Everyone has an opinion on font, it seems! Most writers are aware that the classic and most used font is Times New Roman in a 10- or 12-point size. This is typically the requirement for most types of submissions—from submissions to agents, to magazines and other journals, and to many editors. That being said, it doesn't need to be the font that is chosen for your paperback book, however.

Most typesetters have favorite fonts and will use different fonts for different genres, but most will agree that when formatting for a paper book, a serif font is preferable for the body text.

> **Note**: A serif font has letters with little feet—extra lines to add texture to the letter. A sans-serif font is smooth and lacks the grounding or extra bases to the letters.

I've included a number of articles about choosing fonts in the Appendix of this book. We'll use this section to talk in generalities and I'll leave you to read the articles about specifics. Typically a paperback is formatted in a serif font and an electronic book is formatted in a sans-serif font. Remember, one of the classic rules of formatting is that readers shouldn't notice it. Anything that draws the reader's focus away from the storyline is a bad thing.

Because of this, you want to make sure that your book fits within accepted norms. Don't choose a really cool font that results in your readers having difficulty reading your story. You might choose that really cool font for headings, for chapter titles but choose a more classic font for the body text. It is fairly normal to have at least two fonts used in the formatting of paper books as described—one for titles and one for body.

Pick up that paperback book again and count the number of lines of text on a page. As I mentioned above, in a book with a trim size of 6X9 inches, there will be somewhere between 30 and 35 lines of text per page. If your trim size is smaller, there will be fewer lines. You don't want text that is single-spaced, like in an essay, as it will be more difficult to read. A typical starting point for text is a little bit more than single-spaced— something like 1.15. When choosing a font, choose one that is easy to read and again, gives the book the appearance of space, not the appearance of being cramped. If you are reading this book in the paperback version, I typically format in Garamond 12 point or Times New Roman 12 point. Those are my preferences, but test out a number of fonts, read some articles I've listed at the back of this book and see what would work best for you. Ultimately, as you'll find out in the next chapter, depending on what tool you use to format your book, you may be limited in the choices you have. Whatever font and font size you choose will be set in stone in a PDF and then be reflected in the print copy.

Electronic books, however, are a different story. If you remember back to your homework of playing with reading devices and apps, you'll realize that you have very little control over what font your electronic book is viewed in. Either the person reading your book goes with whatever the preset is (they may not know how to change it) or the settings have been changed, and the book will be viewed in the font that the reader has chosen. That doesn't mean that you shouldn't consider some style options when formatting your electronic book, just that font type and size are not all that important.

Odds & Ends

In this last section, we will talk about the bits and pieces of information that don't fit anywhere else—mostly a collection of dos and don'ts.

1) Paper books typically have text that is right and left justified (or double justified). Again, remember that formatting should be invisible to the reader. A book that has text that is only left justified is too far from the norm to be received successfully by readers.

2) Use hyphenation of words to help with spacing issues

in a double justified page. Unless you allow for words to be broken and hyphenated, the formatting program will stretch the words across the page in order to make them fit and results in odd-looking lines of text.

3) New chapters traditionally start on the right-hand side page. This will create some blank left-side pages to compensate. These are normal and should be present.

4) Although page numbers on every page are normal in an essay or many other written documents, it isn't normal in books. Again, go back and look at your paperback book and you'll find that there are no page numbers on title pages, copyright pages and blank pages (at the end of a chapter for example). Page numbers may also be absent on chapter start pages when placed at the top of the page. Controlling page number placement is something I struggle with when working with Word. This is one of the primary reasons that I use another method of formatting. We will be talking more about methods of formatting in the next chapter.

5) Like page numbers don't belong on blank pages, header text also does not belong on blank pages. It also doesn't belong on title pages or chapter start pages.

6) The first numbered page of your book should be a right-facing page and numbering should start with the number 1 (whether it is displayed or not). This page is likely a chapter start page or something similar. If you choose to put page numbers on some of your front matter pages, they should be Roman numerals and in italics.

7) If you choose to use an image or images in your book —an image that represents your publisher's logo, a little image that decorates each chapter start page or an image that is inserted within the text, ensure that all these images are 300 dpi when creating a paper version of your book. Anything less will produce a fuzzy unprofessional look. That level of resolution isn't as important when creating an

electronic version of your book, as most reader screens don't display above a resolution of 72 dpi.

Now that we have talked about the structure, let's talk about formatting, aka converting a Word document into other formats.

FORMATTING

In the previous chapter we covered the structure of a book—what is literally needed when putting a final product together. In this chapter we are going to talk about the array of tools available to get the formatting job done. To direct your attention back a few chapters, you'll remember that I listed the four file types you need. To refresh, they are— .doc/.docx, .mobi, .epub and .pdf.

In the modern world of publishing, "publishing" involves uploading files on various websites, perhaps waiting for files to be converted into the desired format, waiting for these files to go through some sort of a verification or approval process and then waiting until the final product is live. You might notice that each step involves the word "wait."

A key point I want to emphasize before we move further is that most retailer websites will convert a file for you. Most of the retailers that we deal with as authors will take a Word document (.doc or .docx) as the starting point and convert it to the format needed for that particular retailer.

I choose to not do this for several reasons. The first and

primary reason is that Word is not my friend and frequently I am heard swearing like a trucker when trying to deal with Microsoft Word. My hat is off to those of you who can ~~wrestle a Word document to the floor~~ manage Word and make it do what you want it to do. When I get a Word doc to the point where it is "finished" I find the conversion process doesn't produce a nice-looking end product. I like to blame the conversion process carried out by the various retailers, but I'm sure that I'm ~~mostly~~ partly to blame with my Word skills.

My choice is to create all the files that are required and only upload the file type that is required. In addition to my dislike of Word, I'm quite particular about how the final product looks. When I create all the final products, I know what they are going to look like when live on a retail site and available for sale. When I rely on what is often an automated process to create the various files, I've not been happy with the final product.

Back to the point of this chapter—to help you understand all the common options that are available to create your various file formats. In the section below I've listed the common methods/programs of formatting, how to access and a few comments about each. Before we start down this path of describing the various programs, the best thing you can do for yourself (and your sanity) is to ensure that you are starting with as clean a Word document as possible. We covered a few tips and tricks in a previous chapter.

Before we talk about the commercial products available to change a Word document into another file type to be used in publishing, I want to emphasize that it is possible to use a clean, well-organized Word document for the creation of e-books as well as paper books. Because of that, we will start our discussion with Microsoft Word.

Microsoft Word

Many purists in the Indie world would never consider using anything but Word to format their books. I will never be that person; however, if you want to be that person there is quite a bit of help available.

So, what do I mean when I say format a book using Microsoft Word? This means adjusting the page size to match your chosen trim size. It means setting the margins (and justification) and gutter properly (especially when considering a print book). It means putting proper paragraph styling in place (not using the tab button) and choosing the font(s) you would like to use. It means putting headers, footers and page numbers in place on the proper pages (and missing where they should be missing.) It means putting in proper chapter starts in place and associated blank pages to force uniformly right-facing chapter starts. Finally, it means including all the architecture of a traditional book as discussed in a previous chapter. If this is in your skill set, my hat is off to you. But please be aware that there is help available—quite a bit of it.

As you will see in the next chapter when we talk about the various retailers, it is possible to take a clean, well-formatted Word document and allow the retailer to create the file version they want. As I said above, this isn't a skill I have, and I've not seen a final product that I like, but I'm pretty picky! That being said, many authors use a properly formatted Word document as the only manuscript file and are very happy with the result.

Let's talk about the help available to authors wanting to venture into this world. In the appendix of this book please find links to several tutorials as well as the requirements of the various retailers for condition of the file that is uploaded. These links along with some YouTube videos should have you moving in the right direction!

If you are comfortable with Word but need a bit of extra help, KDP Print has Word templates that can be downloaded for free that many authors have used over the years. These templates set all the style parameters on Word and then the manuscript can either be copy and pasted in or the author can create the book directly using the templates.

There are also premium templates available from The Book Designer, aka Joel Friedlander, as well as other places. I have referenced Joel in this book, and several references to his site can be found in the Appendix. Joel has many years of formatting experience and has a wonderful site that is chock full of information. He cares about the little details of book formatting. He recognizes the struggles that authors have and has created a series of templates. These premium templates can be purchased from his site for either Word or InDesign. Most templates bring a specific style into play, which is appropriate for each genre/project type. Joel's templates can be purchased for three trim sizes—5.25" x 8", 5.5" x 8.5" and 6" x 9". The margins have been set for print on demand, the architecture pages have been created and the headers and footers are set. I have used Joel's templates and although I wouldn't use the word easy, the support he provides is very thorough. If you are comfortable with Word and want to head in this direction, I strongly recommend these templates. The link to the templates can be found in the Appendix. Also find links to YouTube videos to guide you visually through the use of these templates in the Appendix.

If you are not really comfortable with Word or simply want to create the individual file formats that the various retailers can use for your end product, there are a large number of choices. Listed below are choices that exist at the beginner or intermediate level (and marked as such). What are listed below are either websites or programs that can be downloaded onto your computer. There are choices available that aren't listed below, but either they aren't commonly used or require what I would consider to be advanced skills.

1) Pressbooks (http://pressbooks.com)

Pressbooks describes itself as a *"…simple book production software."* They go on to say: *"…import an existing manuscript, choose a book design theme, and export into all the file formats you need to publish your books: PDF, MOBI, EPUB, and other XML formats."*

This is a premium service, which runs $19.99USD for an e-book conversion or $99.00USD for e-book and print as of this printing. This fee is per book. Pressbooks allows for a manuscript to be imported or each chapter can be copied and pasted into the program. An author can choose a theme and even store the files for future changes once the next book is created.

Since Pressbooks is a website, it doesn't matter what kind of computer you have and since they retain your book files, you are protected against file loss if your personal computer has issues. Pressbooks is a relatively straightforward site to use. It is considered to be a beginner level program.

2) Calibre (http://calibre.com)

Calibre is described as an E-book Manager. An interesting, yet appropriate label. Calibre can store and allow for reading of multiple formats of e-books. It is a program that runs on a desktop or laptop computer and works easily on

Mac as well as PC devices. This program serves as an e-book viewer/reader as well as a storage program for e-books and is often referred to as an e-reader program. It allows reading of e-books as well as magazines and other items downloaded from the Internet.

Calibre has been around for more than a decade, having launched in late 2006. It is a free, open source program that is available in about 200 countries and has been translated into a dozen languages.

We're interested in Calibre in this section for its format-ting capabilities. Calibre will allow a file to be uploaded (.doc, .mobi, .epub, PDF and others) and will allow editing of that file. It will then allow conversion of that file to a different file type (.doc, .mobi, .epub, .PDF among the many choices) and allows for export of the file. Since Calibre combines the conversion function at the same point as the reading/testing function, many authors are fond of using Calibre for formatting. One of the common complaints and one thing that turned me off Calibre many years ago is the introduction of artifacts into the text. An artifact can be defined as a weird character(s) that appears within the text of an ePub or mobi file that wasn't visible in the Word doc.

Calibre is an open source program and is actively supported and updated. It has been a while since I have heard any significant complaints about artifacts. I also think that authors are getting better and better at creating a clean Word document to format from. It is fairly common knowl-edge that non-typical characters used in the creation of a manuscript can often result in odd characters in the end product. This brings up another reason to carefully proof the final formatted product before releasing it for sale.

3) Scrivener (https://www.literatureandlatte.com/)

The folks at Literature & Latte created Scrivener over a

decade ago. It was created to help in the process of writing long texts—by writers for writers. According to their website, the staff at Literature & Latte don't like to think of themselves as a software company, but they are! Scrivener is a piece of software that can be used on a Mac or PC or even a mobile device for writers on the go. It is a piece of software that is actively worked on and supported.

Scrivener is primarily known as a content-generation tool or writing tool for writers. It allows writers to write their novel, collect research, order bits and pieces of ideas, create character sketches, create scene sketches among many other cool functions. I often use Scrivener to write the first draft of my books. I do a ton of research beforehand and Scrivener allows me to keep files of my research. What I really love about Scrivener is the ability to write a book with a split screen—the content that I'm generating on one side of my computer screen and my pages of research on the other. No flipping back and forth from document to document.

I attended a workshop on how to use Scrivener for fiction writers a few months ago and was amazed at the tagging, color coding and plotting capabilities that Scrivener has. For the writer of fiction, it seems that the possibilities are endless.

But we are talking about formatting in this chapter. Many fans of Scrivener use it for more than just writing. Writers can print from Scrivener as well as export a wide variety of files—Microsoft Word, RTF, PDF, HTML, ePub and mobi.

Part of the workshop that I attended several months ago involved a demonstration of the export process. Although it seemed a bit involved at first glance, the end product that it produced was quite nice. If you are interested in using Scrivener to format, I suggest you watch one of the videos in the Appendix and decide if this is something that you are interested in doing. I've also included links to the presenter at the workshop I attended and her courses. Formatting using Scrivener is not something that I would consider to be at the beginner level.

4) Jutoh (http://www.jutoh.com)

Although Jutoh is one of the lesser known programs used for formatting, it has its fans. Jutoh is a program that works on Macs as well as PCs and is an:

> "...Inexpensive piece of software that allows you to take a Word document and compile it into e-book and mobi formats." (From Jutoh site)

At the time of this writing, the program is $39.00US and available from the link above. To be clear, I've never used Jutoh, but do work with a number of authors who are huge fans and would use nothing else. There are tutorials available on the site that provide a nice overview of the program. I have included a number of YouTube videos in the references section. These videos will give you a good idea of whether this is a program that you can manage or not. Having tried several programs over the years, I would consider this program to have an intermediate level of difficulty. You need to be able to manipulate files and find and eliminate compiling errors.

5) Sigil

Sigil is a free, open-source ePub editor that allows writers to create an ePub file that can be uploaded to most retailers. At one point I used Sigil and although I liked it at the time, I was quick to switch when I found a simpler tool. Sigil is considered to be the free—and not as well supported —version of its distant cousin Jutoh. It will only supply an ePub file at the end and does not supply a mobi or PDF. It is, however, suggested for books that have complicated features such as endnotes, lots of pictures, footnotes and the like. I would consider Sigil to be an intermediate to advanced level program with the expectation to be able to delve into code. I've listed a YouTube video in the references section of this book that, although older, gives a very clear overview of this program.

For people who are very particular about how their ePub file looks and like to be able to tweak the look and feel, Sigil will allow that kind of control.

6) InDesign (https://www.adobe.com/ca/)

InDesign is an Adobe program that can be accessed through a subscription program. It is a program that will work equally well on a Mac or PC.

Graphic designers and authors can access InDesign by subscription as of this writing for either $19.99/month if paid once a year or $29.99/month paid by month.

Adobe InDesign is considered to be the first choice for professional designers and many graphic artists. This software allows the combination of text and graphics to be laid out on pages of any size. Most will agree that this software, although very powerful, has a steep learning curve.

InDesign is the gold standard for creating a PDF as the basis of a print copy of a book. Although I enjoyed the technical challenge of learning InDesign, it would take me about six to eight hours to create a finished PDF. I have found a faster option.

7) Vellum (https://vellum.pub/)

Vellum is my method of formatting and has been for several years. It is quickly becoming the go-to tool of Indie authors. Although it was originally created to generate e-books, its most recent advancement involved moving into the print world with the creation of a print-ready PDF as well as the e-book files.

To quote from the Vellum blog of how it came to be developed:

> "We realized that part of the problem was the tools being used, tools that had typically been designed for the printed page. E-books were much different.
>
> And that's when we realized we could create something better. We wanted to build a tool that was designed for e-books; from small details like chapter navigation to unique features like built-in knowledge of store requirements. We wanted to bring the richness of print books to the digital world with stylized headings and typesetting that followed standards of book design. Most of all we wanted to give authors and publishers things they'd likely never experienced when creating e-books: ease-of-use, predictability, and sometimes a bit of fun." ~Vellum website blog

This premium formatting tool is only available for Mac computers; however, it can be used with Mac In Cloud technology https://www.macincloud.com/ (a service that allows a user to rent Mac functionality by the hour or month).

Vellum allows for the import of a Word document and the generation of an e-book properly formatted for each retail site within a very short period of time. It includes classic little touches like custom drop caps and ornamental flourishes, the ability to easily create box sets, have links to Facebook and Twitter in the author bio and even individual store links for readers to purchase books via various bookstores.

I love the little touches that come with Vellum as well as the overall ease of creating e-books. I like that Vellum comes with embedded information. It knows the order in which pages should appear. It understands the unique file and cover graphic requirements for the retailers, so I don't have to figure that out. It even figures out the correct margin sizes for print depending on the number of pages. I've included a short YouTube video in the Appendix that demonstrates use of Vellum. It is a method of formatting that I would consider to be at the beginner level.

8) Kindle Create

(https://kdp.amazon.com/en_US/help/topic/G202131100)

Kindle Create is a new tool that has just been released. As of the writing of this book, it is considered to still be in beta, or testing mode. It is a free program available for Mac as well as PC computers. It will take a Word document or a PDF document and convert it into a formatted Kindle e-book. It will detect chapters in the source document and will create a TOC (table of contents). This program will allow the user to choose from a variety of themes as well as viewing before packaging for uploading to Amazon/KDP.

The positive aspect of this program is it will format from a PDF—most programs don't handle PDFs very well. The obvious negative is that it only formats for

Amazon/KDP. For an instructional video from KDP, see the list in the resources section at the back of the book.

9) Amazon Comic Book Creator App

If you are interested in creating a comic book, Amazon has a Comic creator (https://www.amazon.com/gp/feature.html?docId=1001103761)

Comics are not something that are nicely formatted for an e-reader. The images are often poorly displayed and depending on the size of the screen being used to read the comic, it can be a frustrating experience. If your book is along the lines of a comic book, check out this Amazon functionality and see if it will allow you to create the product you envisioned.

Now that we have gotten to this point in the chapter and having read everything that I have shared, you may decide that you are never going to format your own books. I respect that opinion—you aren't alone—many authors choose to hire a service. There are many services that will format your book for you. Before we talk about how to find someone who can do this job for you, let's start with questions to ask.

1) Are there file requirements for submission? Does the formatter want everything in one Word file or the manuscript in a separate file from the copyright information, dedication page? Do they want a separate document that contains information such as trim size, style of headers and footers?

2) Are specific book files produced for each retailer? Or what is the end point/final product?

3) What is the fee? Is there a price break for formatting for e-book as well as print?

4) Are there guarantees of compatibility between the end product and the retailers? (As we'll learn shortly, some of the retailers are pickier than others about the condition of files)

5) Are there extra fees for images, glossaries, etc.?

6) Is there a linked TOC (Table of Contents) for e-books and a page number-based TOC for print?

8) What is the charge for changes?

9) How long are the files kept by the formatter in order for changes to be made (i.e. to the back matter when you publish your next book)?

How to find a formatter?

Now that you have the questions to ask, let's address the question of where to search. Let's go back to my advice to join one or more writer's groups. Many writers' groups have lists of various service providers—from editors to formatters to graphic designers. I know that many of the groups that I belong to will offer suggestions or even have lists of service providers on their websites. It is likely that your editor has contacts also.

If you aren't successful with those suggestions or want to move further afield, I'd suggest that you look at the help documents of the various retailers, aggregators and distributors we will talk about in the next few chapters. Reputable formatters will be clear about the costs as well as what they can and can't do. To get you started, I've included a list of formatting companies in the Appendix of this book.

I'll leave you with a quote from a multi-published author, Jim Giammatteo:

"Layout and formatting are not as easy as they sound. Assuming you plan on offering both e-book and print book versions, that means you have to produce the book in several different formats: MOBI, EPUB and PDF. Not only do you have to ensure the accuracy of these files, you have to also ensure that each file works on as many devices as you can test: Android phones and tablets, iPhones and iPads, computers, Kindles, NOOKs, Kobo readers, etc."

~ *Jim Giammatteo*

IV

WHERE TO SELL
YOUR BOOK

13

WHERE DO YOU SELL YOUR BOOK?

The next stop along the roadmap is to learn where your book can be offered for sale to readers.

Let's take a step back and talk about the assumptions of many beginner authors. They often try to mirror what they feel is the process involved in the traditional publishing world. Since many are aware that traditional publishers print books, have a warehouse or warehouses filled with books and have distributors who "sell" books to bookstores, they envision copying this process.

What happens in the world of indie/self-publishing is we upload a book file to sell at primary sales points and we use print on demand retailers for printing paperback books for sale to readers. We may have some books printed to keep at home with us for in-person sales, but unless in-person events are something we frequently do, we don't keep large numbers of our books at home. We don't distribute paperback books to bookstores or sales channels ourselves so please don't envision having your own mini warehouse of your books at home. In fact if bookstores carry our paperback books, they will order copies through their ordering process. The books will be printed on demand from Amazon or IngramSpark and delivered to the bookstore. It is possible that you will be allowed to leave a few of your books to be sold by consignment at a bookstore. As we will talk about in the last chapter of this book, one of the selling points some self-publishing companies offer is a large number of your books printed and delivered to you. This is not an advantage.

One last comment about print copies of your book. It is possible to have copies of your books printed locally. In some cases, local printers are more cost effective than ordering copies for hand selling from Amazon. Ask for some quotes and compare prices.

In the next few chapters we will discuss various places available to sell your book to readers. We'll follow that up with instructions on setting up accounts and step-by-step instructions on uploading files to various sales points.

14

BOOK RETAILERS

Under the banner of "Where do I sell my book?" we are going to look at Retailers as well as Aggregators and Distributors. And yes, we'll be defining some terms and adding some new words to your vocabulary.

As I'm sure you have gathered as we have made our way through this book, there are a wide variety of places where your book can be sold. When talking to most beginner authors, they envision their book for sale in their local bookstore. As you'll see shortly, there are many more choices than the local bookstore.

The primary retailers for books, both worldwide, as well as in Canada are:

- Amazon
- Kobo
- iTunes/iBooks
- Barnes & Noble
- GooglePlay

When listing the minor retailers, I was personally astonished at the list I was able to put together! I've created an Appendix that shows all the major and minor retailers and how to make your book available in various locations.

I'm going to use this chapter to explain what and who each of the major retailers are as well as some details about them. Many of you will be familiar with Amazon, for example, but may find some unfamiliar retailers on the list.

One last point before I start the list. As I'm sure you will become aware as we go through the lists in the next two chapters, there are choices to be made. Where to offer your book for sale? What are the advantages or disadvantages of various choices? We'll get there! Once I explain the players in the game, I'll explain some of the finer points of the choices.

Amazon

Let's start with a great quote from Britannica.com - the online version of Encyclopedia Britannica:

> "Amazon.com is a vast Internet-based enterprise that sells books, music, movies, housewares, electronics, toys, and many other goods, either directly or as the middleman between other retailers and Amazon.com's millions of customers. Its Web services business includes renting data storage and computing resources, so-called "cloud computing," over the Internet. Its considerable online presence is such that, in 2012, 1 percent of all Internet traffic in North America traveled in and out of Amazon.com data centres.
>
> The company also makes the market-leading Kindle e-book

readers. Its promotion of these devices has led to dramatic growth in e-book publishing and turned Amazon.com into a major disruptive force in the book-publishing market."

Amazon is definitely the big gorilla in the room! Amazon was incorporated in 1994 and started its life as an online bookstore. As we see from the quote above, they quickly evolved from selling books to selling a huge number of items via their various (initially) online locations. Although Amazon started out as Amazon.com, in the years since that start, Amazon has moved into other countries creating country/geography specific sites:

Amazon.ca (Canada)

Amazon.co.uk (UK)

Amazon.cn (China)

Amazon.co.jp (Japan)

Amazon.com.sg (Singapore)

Amazon.fr (France)

Amazon.de (Germany)

Amazon.it (Italy)

Amazon.nl (Netherlands)

Amazon.es (Spain)

Amazon.com.mx (Mexico)

Amazon.com.au (Australia)

Amazon.com.br (Brazil)

Although Amazon started by selling books, books now make up a very small percentage of their bottom line. Many of you will be aware that Amazon recently purchased Whole Foods, but were you aware that they own Audible, Goodreads and over 40 other companies?

What is convenient is once our books are uploaded they will be available for sale on all the various iterations of Amazon. Let's talk about that upload for a sec. We can actually use a number of different entry points for a number of different types of book products.

In a few chapters from now we will talk strategy, but for now, we'll just describe the various parts of Amazon that we will deal with with respect to publishing and talk strategy later.

The two main arms of Amazon are Kindle Direct Publishing (KDP) which can be found at http://kdp.com and ACX which can be found at http://acx.com. Historically, print on demand books were created through Create-Space, but quite recently Amazon has moved that function to KDP Print.

KDP is historically where we have uploaded a mobi file to create a Kindle book. More recently this part of Amazon has been dabbling in the creation of paperback books. By the time you read this book, all CreateSpace books will have been migrated over to KDP. CreateSpace will cease to exist at some point over this year. ACX is the arm of Amazon that deals with audiobooks. For several years, ACX was the only player in the audio game. We'll discuss more about audiobooks in a future chapter. Regardless of what is uploaded where, all these portals lead to products being available for sale in all of the Amazon stores. In other words, regardless of what country you come from, you will deal directly with Amazon.com via kdp.com. If you are Canadian, you don't deal with Amazon.ca, likewise if you are from the UK, you don't deal directly with Amazon.co.uk. By uploading to one location, your books will automatically be available for purchase in all 14 Amazon stores.

Where and what you upload involves choices and strategies—which we will discuss in a future chapter.

Royalties

The amount of royalties that Amazon pays depends on a number of factors: sale price, delivery cost, and production cost.

Let's start with e-books. KDP pays royalties of 70% of sale price for books priced from $2.99 to $9.99, or 35% for books priced under $2.99 generally speaking. There are some countries that pay 35% regardless of the price point unless the book is enrolled in KDP Select (which is explained in a future chapter). If the book file that you are selling is large, there may be a delivery cost subtracted from the royalties you receive. A book that is very long (think epic fantasy) or contains images, will create a file that is larger than "average." KDP pays royalties (usually) as a direct deposit to your bank account once a month with a two-month delay. In other words, you are paid for books that are sold two months after the sale is final.

KDP Print royalties depend on a number of factors and isn't as clearcut as with e-books. They pay 60% minus printing costs. If a book is priced at $15.00 and the printing costs are $4.85, the royalty paid is $4.15.

$(0.60 \times 15) - 4.85 = 4.15$

The numbers are a bit different for expanded distribution (explained below) Amazon pays 40% royalties instead of the 60% mentioned above.

Expanded Distribution

Although we are going to talk about distribution in the next chapter, I wanted to mention "expanded distribution" before moving on to the next retailer. Most of the primary retailers that we will talk about in this chapter do more than make your book available for sale at their location. Most will have some sort of expanded distribution in place. In other words, they will make your book available for sale in other retailer locations, in other what I call secondary locations. In the Appendix, please find a list of all primary retailers and locations they distribute to. In a future chapter we will be talking about Distributors and Aggregators and this topic will come up again.

Kobo

Kobo is often thought of as the Canadian online retailer. In fact, Kobo makes electronic books available in over 200 countries, either directly or via partnerships. If you look closely at the logo at Kobo's landing page, you'll realize that the name has changed to Rakuten Kobo because of a relatively recent merger. In the publishing world, we still refer to this site as Kobo, however.

Kobo only sells e-books (ePubs) and in fact they have their own reading devices and apps—as you may be aware because of one of your first homework assignments.

On the home page of the Kobo site can be found the following quote:

> *"At Kobo, we embody everything you love about your favourite local bookshop, perfected for your modern life. Our mission is to bring the power of reading to your world — because we're booklovers, just like you. Why do we do it? Because we believe stories shape who we are, and words can enhance and transform the world around us."*

They claim to have five million titles available for sale and offer a points system, a type of reward system to encourage readers to keep coming back to them.

Although your books will appear for sale on Kobo, the point of upload is what's called Kobo Writing Life (kobowritinglife.com). Any books that are uploaded to Kobo Writing Life can be made available on some of the minor retail sites through agreements between Kobo and their partners. In this way, Kobo can be considered to be a retail site as well as an aggregator or distributor. We will discuss aggregators and distributors in the next chapter and a complete list of Kobo's partner sites can be found in the Appendix.

Royalties

Kobo pays through EFT (Electronic Funds Transfer) directly to your bank account. Authors are paid 45 days after the end of each month that they have met the minimum threshold of $50USD. For books that haven't met the threshold, authors receive payment every 6 months. In terms of royalties, they pay 70% of the list price for every book $2.99 and over. Books priced below $2.99 receive 45% of the list price.

iTunes/iBooks

The next retail site we'll talk about is iTunes/iBooks. And yes, there is a bit of name confusion. Many authors are a bit confused as to the relationship between iTunes and iBooks. Here's a quote from iTunes that will help with clarity:

"Users can download and access iBooks through iTunes, and once logged in, the iBooks app connects users to the iBookstore, an online book store with a selection of more than 700,000 paid and free books. iBooks also integrates with Apple's iCloud service, enabling users to access books purchased or downloaded through iBooks on all of their iOS devices."

iTunes/iBooks is one of the retail sites with which authors can frequently struggle. In order to access the upload portal for this retailer, you need to use a program called iTunes Producer to upload your book files to iTunes. As I'm sure you assumed, iTunes producer is only available for a Mac. If you don't have a Mac, you need to use another way to have your books available on this retailer. As you will see in the next chapter, there are many other ways to get your book in iTunes/iBooks other than direct upload.

Although many authors grumble about this platform, it makes books available directly in a large number of countries.

The list is currently: Argentina, Australia, Austria, Belgium, Bolivia, Brazil, Bulgaria, Canada, Chile, Colombia, Costa Rica, Cyprus, Czech Republic, Denmark, Dominican Republic, Ecuador, El Salvador, Estonia, Finland, France, Germany, Greece, Guatemala, Honduras, Hungary, Ireland, Italy, Japan, Latvia, Lithuania, Luxembourg, Malta, Mexico, Netherlands, New Zealand, Nicaragua, Norway, Panama, Paraguay, Peru, Poland, Portugal, Romania, Slovakia, Slovenia, Spain, Sweden, Switzerland, United Kingdom, United States, Venezuela.

I feel it is important to consider the millions and millions of readers with an iPhone or iPad on which the iBook app comes preinstalled. For those folks who struggle with technology, iBooks is one of the easiest reading apps to use. It is already installed on the device and once the reader enters their Apple credentials, they can shop for books right from the app. There is no need to figure out how to get an e-book ready to read, or get the app on the device. It is quite seamless.

Royalties

In terms of royalties, iTunes pays 70% on all titles regardless of price and they deposit the funds through EFT to your bank account.

Barnes & Noble

As it's commonly referred to, B&N is an American soil, bricks-and-mortar bookstore. It is also an online store selling both e-books and paperback books. It has a reading app that is only available through the American or EU iTunes or the American or EU version of GooglePlay store. B&N also sells an e-reader device called a Nook. Both the app and the Nook allow online shopping and direct delivery to the reader or app. The downfall is B&N makes it awkward to obtain the app or the Nook when you live outside of the US or certain EU countries. Again, because I have a US PO box, I had my Nook delivered to my US PO Box many years ago when I purchased it.

Uploading directly to B&N is only available to US residents and residents of UK, France, Italy, Germany, Spain, The Netherlands and Belgium. I also believe that payments can only be made to banks on US or EU soil although that isn't specifically stated on their website. For many years I've had an American soil bank account and also early on in my publishing career I needed to get an EIN tax number from the IRS in order to be paid by Amazon. Those two, combined with my US PO box, and I was able to publish directly on B&N. The EIN is no longer required on Amazon and if you don't live near the US like I do, there are easier ways to get your books into B&N using aggregators or distributors, as we'll discuss in the next chapter.

The upload site for Barnes & Noble is NookPress.com. Authors can upload files to sell e-books and print books. The prices for printing are not as competitive as those from KDP Print. The NookPress site states:

Bestselling authors are eligible to pitch their book to B.&N store buyers and host store events and book signings.

This, of course insinuates that if authors aren't bestsellers, they don't qualify. If this is something that interests you, I encourage you to enquire.

Royalties

B&N has an interesting royalty structure. They pay 40% on books priced between 99 cents and $2.98, 60% on books priced between $2.99 and $9.99 and 40% on books priced over $10.00. Authors are paid when they have accrued $10.00 in royalties and are paid 60 days after the close of the calendar month in which the sale occurs. The example that is given on the B&N site is if you receive sales in August, you will be paid for them in October. All royalties are deposited directly into a bank account.

GooglePlay

The last primary retailer from the list above is Google-Play, a Google product. GooglePlay only deals in e-books and the books can be accessed in a variety of ways. Most phones can load a GooglePlay app and anyone with a

Google account or a Gmail account can access GooglePlay. There are two major ways to have books available for sale on GooglePlay—either you need to be invited to open an account or you use an aggregator/distributor to offer your books for sale there. I'm sure you'll hear complaints over time from authors who run afoul of Amazon because of something that GooglePlay does. As we'll talk about in a future chapter, according to Amazon's rules, your book must not be available anywhere else for a cheaper price. GooglePlay tends to be fond of discounting books without warning—and if Amazon notices, you can get in trouble.

Royalties

GooglePlay pays 52% royalties once a month and usually within the first week or so of the month following the sale.

Now that we've covered the primary retail points, we need to discuss what I would consider secondary retail points. I've listed all the secondary retailers and their associated distributor in an Appendix of this book. We aren't going to take the time and explain who is who, and who does what. For your purposes, your sales will occur in a small number of locations, mostly primary retailers.

I will, however, point out who a few of these secondary retailers are.

There are several big services that supply books to libraries—either public, elementary/secondary school or post secondary. Examples are: Askews & Holts, Overdrive, Yuzu, Axia360, and Bibliotheca. Although many indie authors get their local library to carry their book by taking in a few copies and donating them, libraries do buy books! Drop by your local library and find out who they get their books from so that you can make sure that your books are available from that service.

IngramSpark, Gardner, WH Smith and Bertram are significant print retailers, either at the wholesale level or at the bricks-and-mortar level. Finally Scribd is an example of a subscription service. Readers pay a fee and they read what they choose. A similar service is offered from Amazon. (Kindle Unlimited) Several years ago, there were several subscription services and since then some doors have been closed. Time will tell if this type of service will die off or pop up in some other form.

In the next chapter we will move on to talk about companies that make your book available for sale in other locations than their own.

15

DISTRIBUTORS & AGGREGATORS

As self-published authors, we don't have access to some of the channels the traditional publishers have, at least not directly. Over the years, work-arounds have been discovered or created. The people or businesses that traditional publishers use to sell their books to bookstores are generally off limits, but businesses have cropped up that serve as distributors. For self-publishers, when we talk about distribution, we are mostly concerned with e-book distribution. If you remember what Data Guy had to say on the subject of self-published print book sales:

> "Self-published authors have quickly figured out that print books are more expensive to create, they can't compete effectively in bookstores as they rarely get shelf space, and even when they do, they often lose money. They have migrated toward venues where they can compete more effectively for sales with less risk— electronic books."

In this chapter we are going to talk about the various channels available to get books into various places—places that aren't what I consider a primary retailer but may distribute to a primary retailer. We are also going to talk about sites where we can upload a Word document and have it converted to other types of files—mobi, ePub, and maybe pdf—and then distributed to various retailers for sale. Honestly, this is the part of the publishing process that many authors struggle to wrap their head around. So many choices are available and since most don't do the same thing, comparing costs and comparing choices becomes difficult to do. This chapter will clarify these topics.

Distribution in the traditional publishing world refers to the process and logistics of getting your book to the consumer. A myriad of services and platforms exist from Amazon to IngramSpark to iBooks, that help you put your work in the hands of readers. Each one has pros and cons.

Let's start the discussion with two definitions - Aggregator and Distributor:

Aggregator - From the dictionary, aggregated or aggregating as a verb can be defined as: to bring together; collect into one sum, mass or body. Looking at the examples from the dictionary, they refer to the collection of services for repackaging and disbursement.

For the purpose of this book, we will define an **aggregator** as a service that takes your manuscript/finished file, converts it to the various digital formats needed for e-book distribution (if you don't upload final files) and delivers your book file to various retail outlets. The Aggregators we will talk about in this chapter will make your print books available to various retail outlets also. Many Aggregators will have partnerships with retail outlets that self-published authors have difficulty accessing on their own. In addition to making your book available to various retail outlets, they will handle all the accounting and payment of royalties to the author. They typically either charge a fee for their service or take a percentage of royalties. More on royalties and fees in a bit.

Distributor - Is the term that typically applies to a middleman used by traditional publishers to get paperback/hardcover books into bookstores. There used to be a clear distinction between Distributors and Aggregators; that line is now blurred. Some distributors also serve as aggregators and vice versa. As you saw when we went through the list of primary retailers, many will act as distributors to partners.

Rather than getting caught up in trying to label services as either one or the other or both, let's just list all the major services available and talk about what they do, where they send books and how much they charge. Once I've outlined all the choices, I'll share my favorites and the reason they are favorites.

Many companies act both as publishers and distributors, producing books as well as making them available to various retail venues. The majority of these distributors are actually wholesalers, passive suppliers who only respond to book orders, as

opposed to active distributors who have a sales team dedicated to placing book orders with retailers
   ~ ALLi

Smashwords

Smashwords is the original e-book distributor. They deal only in e-books and not paperbacks. Created by Mark Corker in 2008 with the goal of making it easy and fast for a writer anywhere in the world to publish an e-book. Smashwords was the first of its kind—truly making it feasible for Indie Authors from any country to access the publishing world. I'll remind you that retailers like Barnes & Noble only accept submissions from the continental US and some EU countries and upload to iTunes requires a Mac. Smashwords provides a way around these issues.

Smashwords serves as an aggregator as well as a distributor, as it will take a well-formatted Word document and convert it to an ePub file. Once an ePub is formed and approved, it can be distributed to a wide variety of other retailers as listed in the Appendix. There are authors who don't like what Smashwords calls their "Meat-Grinder" process of converting a Word document to an ePub, but because they also accept an ePub, you can bypass the conversion process.

In terms of file acceptance, Smashwords will accept a Word document and an ePub; they don't accept a PDF for submission. On their FAQ page:

(https://www.smashwords.com/about/supportfaq) they offer extensive help in not only formatting the Word document, but also offer very detailed explanations on a wide variety of subjects with regard to publishing on Smashwords. In fact, during the research for this book, I'd say that they have the most extensive FAQ of any of the retailers or aggregators that I have listed here.

Authors love Smashwords for their coupon service. This service allows authors to create coupons that can be handed out to readers to get free review copies of books, or books that are a certain percentage off. This is a handy function both when trying to get free review copies to readers as well as to offer deals to some readers, but not all.

Royalties

Smashwords pays royalties monthly, about 30 to 40 days after the close of each calendar month. It will pay via check (for earnings over $75) or PayPal for any royalties over a penny. The amount they pay will depend on where the book is sold. Generally, authors will receive 85% of the net sales proceeds of their books for books sold on Smashwords. Authors will earn 60% of the list price for sales through the distribution network with library sales typically earning 45% of list price. Authors are required to supply tax information to avoid Smashwords withholding 30% for the IRS. Since I'm Canadian I'm familiar with my benefits. Canada is a treaty country with the US, provisions are put in place to allow us to pay tax on our royalties to our tax department. Many other countries are also what are considered to be "treaty" countries and are treated in a similar fashion. Other will be required to have some tax withheld. Smashwords has a brief explanation of these rules here:

https://www.smashwords.com/about/supportfaq#ITIN. For a great source of information on this topic, I'll direct you to an Amazon help page as I feel they have the best explanation.

(https://kdp.amazon.com/en_US/help/topic/G201274690)

Draft2Digital

Draft2Digital is a website that can take a variety of file types and produce an ePub and/or PDF for download or distribution to a variety of partner sites. They don't offer cover art creation, editing or other promotion services, but do have a resources page for recommended partners. They focus on file creation, distribution and sales tracking.

They accept .doc, .docx, or .rtf files for upload to conversion. They also accept a converted/formatted .epub file. As I've mentioned several times, I'm pretty picky about the look of my final product and have never used Draft2Digital's conversion process. What I do like is D2D's unique ability to separately add front and back matter, allowing for easy update of past books once you release new ones. Depending on your chosen method of formatting, the changing of the front and back matter can be an onerous job. Draft2Digital has put measures into place to make this easier. However, if you, like me, choose to upload a fully formatted ePub, you can't take advantage of these features.

Draft2Digital currently distributes to a handful of sites listed in the Appendix of this book and are always looking to add more retailers to their list of partners. Authors have the choice of which of the list of available partners they choose to distribute to—it isn't a one size fits all situation. Likewise, you can control the territories you choose to distribute to, but like many other sites, your retail price is based on a set price in US dollars.

Royalties

There are no upfront charges—even for their conversion process to ePub or PDF, but they will take 10% of the retail price on sales. Payment is made via Cheque, PayPal, Direct Deposit or Payoneer, with a minimum threshold of $25 for cheques, $20 for Payoneer, and $10.00 for international direct deposit (they are based in the US so any non-American author would likely be included in what is described as an international direct deposit). Payments are made once a month with a delay of 60 days after the end of the month in which the sales happened.

Authors are required to fill out a tax interview to avoid withholding taxes. The process is very similar to what other sites require.

In terms of other requirements, since Draft2Digital is distributing to other retailers, the files that are supplied must meet the requirements for the other retailers. Cover graphics must be a minimum of 1600 X 2400px and either the author must provide an ePub file that will pass the inspection processes, and/or they will produce a similar file from a Word file you upload.

One last point about Draft2Digital is their customer support. Within business hours, authors are welcome to phone with questions. There is email support as well, but in my experience, the help that is received either on the phone or by email is excellent.

Publish Drive

Publish Drive is a combination of aggregator and distributor that is relatively new on the scene and they only deal in e-books. It is supported by venture capital money and has its headquarters in Budapest, Hungary. Since they are one of the new kids on the block there is a lot of excitement around them. They have an impressive number of retail sites and libraries they distribute to. They claim an increase of 300% over last year's business (as of the writing of this book) or 485 million titles added in the previous year.

This service is funded by a percentage of royalties—they take 10% of the digital list price to cover their services.

Quick overview videos are available on their site to show that the dashboard seems quite clear and the upload process is straightforward. PublishDrive recommends that the author convert their book on their own—and directs authors to Sigil, InDesign or Vellum to create an ePub file.

For a fee they will format your book for you. For that service they require one of the following formats: .docx, .indd (InDesign file), .rtf, .html, or PDF. Their site states that the conversion fee is calculated on the complexity, the length of the book and the number of pictures.

Although PublishDrive is the new kid on the block, they are one of the only services open to authors in North America that isn't physically located in North America. And because of their start in Hungary, they are considered to have more European distribution partners than their competitors.

IngramSpark

IngramSpark is a huge company on the publishing landscape. It works with indie authors, small publishers and big traditional publishers. They are considered to be unique, as they provide a one-stop platform for both e-book and print.

Their mission statement holds a place of prominence on their website:

"Simply, to help our customers succeed at self-publishing. To provide easy access to professional-grade, fully integrated, print, digital, wholesale, and distribution services at costs tailored to their unique budgeting needs, through a single source, without ever compromising on quality. To make the world a better place for books of all kinds."

As you can see from the list in the Appendix, IngramSpark has the largest list of distribution partners of any of the services we talk about in this chapter. They offer distribution of multiple formats on multiple continents. They handle a wide range of products also. Everything—from novels, to graphic novels to children's books to business books or textbooks—is handled by them. And unlike KDP Print, they handle hardcover as well as paperback books. Generally speaking, they offer a wider range of trim sizes, paper quality, binding type and so on.

IngramSpark has quite specific requirements for its files as follows:

IngramSpark - print - PDF/X-1a:2001 or PDF/X-3:2002 (created from Acrobat or Indesign) with the file name of isbn_txt.pdf or isbntxt.pdf

IngramSpark e-Book - EPUB 3.0 (can't accept enhanced EPUB 3.0 files) with front cover RGB and a minimum of 600px along longest axis

Authors can create an account, upload files and have them moving around the world in a very short period of time. Unlike many of the other services that we have talked about, this service has an upfront cost. As of the time of this printing, to upload an e-book costs $25.00USD, a print book is $49.00USD and a combination of both formats is $49.00USD. There are charges if changes need to be made to a file.

Let's end this chapter with a quote from the Alliance of Independent Authors' book on Self-Publishing.

"...the distinction between a passive wholesaler and an active, sales-oriented distributor is significant here. Employing an aggregator who boasts of "tens of thousands" of retailers and libraries in their distribution network will not ensure that your book is carried by those retailers; it only ensures that a retailer who asks to purchase that book has the option to do so.

Making your book known to these retailers—and the readers they service—is the goal of the next stage of publishing: marketing and promotion."

~ ALLi

V

HOW TO SET UP
ACCOUNTS

HOW TO SET UP ACCOUNTS

A ll of the accounts that need to be set up to publish your book are free, but as would be expected, all are slightly different in the information they require and the layout of their dashboard.

All of the retailers/distributors/aggregators will want information about you, information necessary to forward your royalties to you, information necessary to avoid the US withholding tax and information about your book.

Before you start the process of opening up the various accounts, the process will go easier if you gather the information that will be needed all in one spot—preferably on a Word document on your computer so that you can simply copy and paste from one to the other to speed things up.

The information you will require:

1) About the author
All the various locations will require personal informa-

tion to open an account. This information will include your legal name/publisher name, mailing and/or street address, and phone number. Even if you plan on using a pen name, you still need to provide your real name/business name at some point as tax information will be collected. You likely pay income taxes to your countries' tax authority under your real name/business name. Have your records match to reduce confusion come tax time.

2) Banking/Payment information

All of the retailers/distributors/aggregators need a way to deliver your royalties to you. As you saw in the previous chapter, they all do this slightly differently. Some will offer several choices with various cutoff points. As we saw, it is possible to have your royalties paid to you by cheque, but only once you accrue a certain dollar figure. If you want more immediate gratification, you can look into making use of direct deposit, a Paypal account, or in some cases a Payoneer account. Paypal and Payoneer are two types of services that will transfer funds from a company to your bank account as well as acting as a sort of online bank account. Give some thought as to your preferences. If you don't have a PayPal account, consider opening one. I find having a PayPal account to be handy.

3) Tax information

Most of the retailers/distributors/aggregators now offer what they call a "Tax Interview." I guess they have decided that trying to get non-Americans to fill out US tax forms wasn't working and they now gently walk authors through the collecting information by asking questions. In my mind, there are two tripping points. You will be asked if you have spent time in the US. Different retailers will ask the question slightly different ways and it can easily be interpreted as being asked if you have had a holiday in the US. The question is not referring to holidays. Generally speaking the answer that most non-American residents give to this question is "No." The second tripping point is the question about whether or not your business is carried out in the US. Many would argue that books sold from Amazon.com are sold in the US and therefore the answer should be yes. However, you are in your home country when the books in question are sold in other countries. So the answer to this question is usually "No" also. As a last note, I have had occasion to phone Amazon in sheer frustration when trying to fill out their Tax Interview. The help that I received was quite helpful!

We'll discuss strategies in another chapter, but the account that you open will be your Amazon/KDP account. The portal is:

http://kdp.com

The next step will be gathering the information that will be used when publishing a book.

VI

INSTRUCTIONS FOR UPLOADING

INSTRUCTIONS FOR UPLOADING

In this chapter we are going to make our second-to-last stop on our roadmap to publishing. We are going to talk about the pieces of information and documents that are needed during the process of uploading your file to retailers/distributors/aggregators, or as we'll call it "Publishing."

I do understand that a lot of the content of this chapter is pretty technical, but I wanted to have one place where you can access all this information when it comes time to do this process. Kind of a one-size-fits-all reference sheet.

Although many of the retailers/distributors/aggregators are very similar in the information they require in order to publish/distribute a book, there are differences. The process goes more smoothly if you are organized and simply have to copy and paste your various details into the appropriate fields. We'll start with a general list of requirements and then point out a few things that are unique to each platform. I'm going to divide the requirements into two sections—the files required and the information required.

File requirements for the primary retailers (for more details see the Appendix)

Amazon

KDP (Kindle Direct Publishing- primarily for electronic version of a book)- will accept .doc, .docx, HTML, mobi, ePub, RTF, Plain Text, KPF (now has Kindle Create – see a previous chapter for an explanation)

Cover graphic - .jpeg/.jpg or .tif/.tiff

KDP Print (for the print copy of a book) - PDF

Cover graphic - PDF (see appendix for link to template creator)

Kobo - will accept ePub, .doc, .docx, .mobi, .odt

Cover graphic - .jpeg/.jpg

Barnes & Noble - .doc, .docx, .txt, .rtf, .htm, .html, .epub

Cover graphic - .jpeg/.jpg

iTunes - .epub 2.0.1 or later

Cover graphic - .jpeg/.jpg

Content requirements

In addition to the book file and the cover graphic file, you will be asked for a number of pieces of information during the process of uploading your book—either directly or via one of the companies we'll talk about in the next chapter. The upload process goes much smoother if you have all the information gathered/created ahead of time and enter the appropriate information in the proper spots. Each retailer has slightly different requirements, but they are all similar. Let's talk about each requirement.

Book Title/Subtitle/Edition/Series

All retailers will ask for some or all of these. There are many experts that will share their thoughts on what makes a good book title. If this is something that you want a bit of help with, find resources in the Appendix of this book.

Author Name/Contributors

Clearly, listing the author's name is an obvious piece of information, but you need to give some thought as to whether or not you want to name contributors to your project. Do you want to name your editor or cover artist, for example? This is not required, but can be a nice thing to do. Some authors feel giving credit to their editor will give their book more cachet, showing that it has been edited.

Author Bio

An author bio is information that is added at different places on different retailers. It should be relatively short (a paragraph or a bit more) and should serve as a friendly introduction to you and your work.

Book Description/Blurb

Every book needs a description. Many refer to this as the back cover copy. Whatever name you give it, it needs to be considered to be part of the sales mechanism of a book. Again, I've listed some references in the Appendix of this book that will help you create the perfect blurb. It is also possible to hire a copywriter to write the blurb for you. I did this for one of my books and found the result to be well worth the money both in terms of the end product as well as the stress relief of not having to do this myself.

Categories/BISAC codes

All books are assigned categories. The number changes from retailer to retailer and the selection also changes. Although what you are entering is based on BISAC codes, it can be described as genres. To do some research, go to Amazon.com or Amazon.ca or your local Amazon site and click in the upper left on Departments and then E-Books & Audible. Scroll down a bit until you can see a list under Kindle books. There is a lot of thought that goes into choosing Categories by many authors. And it goes without saying that there are whole books written about strategies that can be used. Choose categories that are close to the truth that have lower numbers of books. The reasoning behind this is so that you are competing against fewer books to rank in a category. To do more research on this subject, please see the Appendix for some suggestions for further reading. For details on how many categories are allowed on each platform, see further on in this chapter

Keywords/Search words

Again, different retailers allow different numbers of keywords. Aim to create a list of 7-10 as some sites allow a certain number of words and others use character count as the determining factor. Think of Keywords as search words —words that can be used when searching Amazon or other retailers for your book. Again, research has gone into this subject. See the Appendix for further reading.

Age & Grade range/Adult content

Most of the retailers allow the author to enter information about potential audience. If the book is aimed at a younger audience, this age/grade guidance will help categorize it properly. If the book's content is only appropriate for adults, state that also.

ISBN

We've covered quite a bit of information about ISBNs and I'll refer you back to that chapter for more details.

DRM

DRM is the acronym for Digital Rights Management. Proponents of DRM will claim that it prevents piracy of electronic books. A quick Google search will tell you instructions abound about how to get beyond this encryption. What DRM does in practical terms? DRM prevents your readers from moving a copy of your book between their devices. For example, if a reader starts reading a book on a laptop computer and wants to move it to an e-reader to read in bed, DRM may prevent this. Whether or not you enact DRM is a personal decision, but once the decision is made, it can't be changed. I don't feel that enabling DRM will prevent dishonest people from being dishonest—it will just frustrate honest readers. For your reference, I've included several articles for further reading in the Appendix.

Manuscript & E-book cover - this goes without saying

Territories

If we look at the world of Traditional publishing the contract that publishers have authors sign is territory specific and often version specific. As an Indie author, you choose which "territories" to sell to. These territories are typically geographical regions. Unless you have signed a contract somewhere or have reason to exclude certain geographical regions, I suggest that you include all territories to maximize your exposure.

Royalties and Pricing

We've talked about Royalties for each retail site above but haven't talked much about pricing. Like fitting in with the norms in terms of trim size and cover graphics, your book should be priced according to the norms of the genre you write in.

Details that are specific to certain retailers / distributors / aggregators

Amazon

Matchbook

Matchbook is an Amazon functionality. If a reader purchases a paperback version of your book, Matchbook (if checked) will allow that reader to purchase a copy of the Kindle version of your book for $2.99 or less. This is a nice thing to do for your readers.

Book Lending

Another functionality unique to Amazon allows readers to lend your Kindle book to friends or family for 14 days. It will disappear off the Kindle of the borrower after the 14 days is finished. Again, a choice, but a nice thing to do for your readers.

KDP enrollment

We're going to talk about KDP Select in a separate chapter, as it requires more than just a simple explanation.

KDP

As we've covered previously, KDP is the location where you will upload the contents for a Kindle book. This requires a graphic that ideally is 2560px X 1600px but Amazon will accept 1000px X 625px. The ratio of height to width is 1.6:1 (which is different than the other retailers). All of the e-book resolutions only need to be 72 dpi and Amazon is no different. KDP allows for seven keywords to be entered and two categories.

KDP Print

If you remember from above, we are going to use KDP Print to upload information for a paperback book. The cover graphic will be uploaded as a PDF file. It will be sized using the Template Creator (see link in the Appendix) and have a 300 dpi resolution. You will be allowed to choose two categories and seven keywords.

Barnes & Noble or NookPress

If you choose to use B&N directly, the cover graphic that you need to upload is less well described. On their site they claim that the width must be at least 750px and the height be at least 1400px and the file size be no more than 2MB in size. They don't give a ratio description. You will be allowed to choose five categories and keywords to a maximum of 100 characters.

Kobo or Writing Life

Like B&N, Kobo isn't very specific in its cover requirements either. It caps the file size for cover graphic at 5MB and suggests that the width to height ratio be 3:4. You will be allowed to choose three categories and Kobo doesn't currently allow for Keywords.

iTunes

iTunes/iBooks is a bit more prescriptive in their information. A book cover has to be 1600px X 2400px. I haven't seen a file size requirement in my research, but likely it is in the range of the others. iTunes allows for two categories to be submitted and Keywords are capped at five.

Draft2Digital

If you remember, Draft2Digital is not a primary retailer —it will distribute your book to primary retailers as well as secondary sites. Because of that, it needs to be a one-size-fits-all place. It needs the right information for all the various retailers. As such, it will allow you to enter five categories but states that likely only one or two will be used. The minimum cover size is 1600px X 2400px. Draft2Digital allows for what it calls Search Terms, not using the title of

Keywords and doesn't seem to have a word limit or a character limit.

PublishDrive

PublishDrive is similar to both Smashwords and Draft2Digital as it will send your book to a variety of primary retailers and a selection of secondary retailers. (for a complete list see the appendix) Again, because your book is sent a variety of places, the requirements of information and files needs to fit the requirements of all the places it will be sent. The cover requirements state a minimum width of 800px X 1280px (but a recommended size of 1600px X 2560px) and they require an ePub file for the interior of the book.

Smashwords

Smashwords will sell copies of your book directly from their website, but like Draft2Digital, Smashwords will send your book to primary retailers and a healthy selection of secondary retailers. Because of that, its requirements are based on the requirements of other places the book can be sent. Each book is allowed two categories and 10 tags or what other locations will call Keywords. Smashwords also requires a short description as well as a long description for each book—something that is unique from the other platforms. The cover requirements state a minimum width of 1400px but a recommended size of 1600px X 2400px with a ratio of 1.5:1

IngramSpark

Like the previous two companies, IngramSpark also sends books to other locations and must meet the requirements of others. The e-book cover must be a minimum of 1600px X 2560px and authors are allowed to enter three categories. For print, the PDF for the cover graphic needs to be created according to the criteria of the book and they, like KDP Print, offer a handy cover calculator (see the resource section for the link). The PDF must be 300 dpi, CMYK and 180 LPI. As I've mentioned previously, they used to have very rigid rules about how the interior PDF was created, but the only warning that I can find while researching is that it can't easily be created from MS Word.

Please find a lot more details on all the above in the Appendix.

VII

STRATEGIES

STRATEGIES

Congratulations! If you followed the instructions, the last chapter would give you enough information to publish your book. Is your job done? (No, of course not.) Is there anything else to learn? (Yes, of course there is!)

As I said in the beginning of the book, there are many different choices involved in publishing a book. At the beginner level, there are the mechanics of preparing files and uploading them to various locations. Once that is done, there are layers and layers of strategy. In this chapter we will discuss some of the basic layers of strategy.

As we learned from Data Guy's information, the majority of all book sales come from sales on Amazon and the vast majority of sales will occur online. There are some exceptions to this, but when talking about the majority of adult fiction and non-fiction the numbers show this to be true.

Because of this, as indie authors, we focus a lot of attention on Amazon. In the previous chapters we learned how to prepare files and upload to at least a handful of different retailers. The first level of strategy involves focusing on

Amazon or "going wide." In a previous chapter I mentioned KDP Select. We are going to start our strategy session with a discussion of KDP Select.

Pros & Cons of KDP Select

There are so many words and acronyms that are used in publishing that don't exist in normal conversation. In this chapter we're going to learn about what makes KDP Select different from KDP. What is KOLL and what's KENP? What the heck is meant by "going wide"?

Let's start with some definitions:

KDP - Kindle Direct Publishing - the website is KDP.com - this is the arm of Amazon that publishes Kindle books.
KDP Select - is exclusivity to KDP. It is an agreement with KDP in which the author chooses to only sell their e-book on Amazon through KDP. Where print books are offered doesn't matter, as this agreement only has to do with the electronic copy of a book. There is a bit more to KDP Select as we'll find out, but this definition will start us.
KOLL - Kindle Owner's Lending Library - Amazon Prime members (another Amazon membership) can read one book each month as part of their membership.
Kindle Unlimited (KU) - Is a subscription service where Amazon offers readers the chance to read unlimited e-books/magazines and listen to unlimited audiobooks for $9.99/month. KU is available in a select number of countries.
KENP - stands for Kindle Edition Normalized Pages and

this number represents the digital tracking of how many pages the KU customer has read and determines the royalties authors earn from KU and KOLL.

Go Wide - have your book available for sale on more than just Amazon/KDP.

When publishing your book, you have the choice to put your Amazon/KDP book (or Kindle book) into KDP Select for three months at a time. The choice to enter a book into KDP Select can be made when uploading the book to the KDP platform or at any point after that. Once a book has been entered into KDP Select, however, it must remain there for three months and can't be sold anywhere else during this time period. There are other rules as well as benefits. Let me explain.

A book that has been entered into KDP Select can only have 10% of it available as a sample read. This will prevent authors from offering the book in an anthology that is available from all retailers or giving away a copy of this book as an incentive to sign up for a mailing list, for example.

In fact, Amazon will offer the first 10% of a book to anyone as a sample that can be sent to their Kindle reader/app or as part of the Look Inside functionality. As you can see, this rule is a bit misleading to the beginner. Authors may think that the only way that they can take advantage of the Look Inside Functionality is by being in KDP Select— which isn't true.

In terms of advantages, any book that is in KDP Select will automatically get 70% royalties regardless of price point and country of sale. It is also included in Kindle Unlimited (KU) and Kindle Owners' Lending Library (KOLL) and will earn a share of the KDP select global fund based on how many pages KU or KOLL customers read.

Authors in KDP Select also have access to a new set of promotional tools. They can schedule a week long Kindle Countdown Deal (see the Glossary for a definition) for Amazon.com and/or Amazon.co.uk readers once during the three months. They can also offer a free book promotion to readers worldwide once during the three month signup.

With a little research many authors determine that there are mixed feelings about KDP Select. Many authors feel that the compensation for pages read is a pittance and don't find the Countdown deals or the free days of any value. Others will swear by it. Even amongst my 15 books, I find that some do well in KDP Select and some do not. I encourage you to do some reading, test the waters and see what happens for you in KDP Select. It's only for three months. I've included some reading resources in the Appendix to help you learn more.

Let's assume you have decided that you are going to "go wide." How does a beginner author look over the information presented in the last few chapters and decide how to proceed? Do you upload files to every site where you can sell a book? Do you make use of some of the aggregators/distributors? What is best for the creation of paperback books? It is completely understandable when beginner authors become overwhelmed at the choices and struggle to understand what is best, or better yet—what is best for **their** book.

Let's start this discussion with some information about the

various arms of Amazon—a common point of confusion—starting with Kindle Direct Publishing.

Kindle Direct Publishing (KDP)

We upload our mobi file, our Kindle book file, to Kindle Direct Publishing (http://kdp.com)—better known as KDP. With changes that Amazon has made over the years, it is now possible to upload a mobi file to the KDP.com site and make it available as an e-book through Amazon and that mobi file can be used to create a print book, also available from Amazon.

KDP Print

When we finish uploading the files and inputting all the information for our Kindle book we are offered the chance to create a paperback book. Clicking on the appropriate choice will then lead you through the process to upload the files and information to create a POD print book. This print book will be offered along side our kindle version on all Amazon sites as well as what is called Expanded distribution (if that is wanted - see information on IngramSpark).

ACX

One site that can be used to create an audiobook file is ACX (http://acx.com), which is part of Amazon also. We'll talk about ACX and other ways to create an audio book in a separate chapter.

Note: One thing to keep in mind is the books from Amazon are POD books. They are not works of art. They are not equivalent to full color, picture-filled coffee table books. They are functional readable books that are good for genre fiction and most non-fiction.

Step 2 of "going wide" is to decide how to make your book available in all the other locations. Essentially there are two decisions—upload files individually to each primary retailer or make use of a service like Draft2Digital, PublishDrive or Smashwords. Uploading to all primary retailers is difficult for some non-US folks. A Mac is required to upload to iTunes, and Barnes and Noble makes it difficult for non-US or non-UK folks to use directly; however, the author ends up with full royalties. Using Draft2Digital, PublishDrive or Smashwords will take away 10% or so of earned royalties for the convenience of using their platform.

This is a choice you need to make for yourself.

Step 3 is uploading to IngramSpark. Not only does Ingram-Spark have the largest distribution network, but it is often the place the bookstores order from. As discussed, there is a charge to upload to IngramSpark and more importantly, they charge for changes. What most authors do is upload their PDF to KDP Print, order a proof copy, and make any changes that are necessary. They then upload the PDF that they know is absolutely correct to IngramSpark and avoid the charge for changes.

One of the pieces of homework I assigned earlier was to go into your local bookstore and ask where they order books. We're going to come back around to that information now. From our list, the two choices that will deal with paperbacks are KDP Print and IngramSpark. Historically, traditional publishers have granted booksellers the right to return unwanted or overstocked copies of books. In fact many booksellers will not stock books that are not returnable. By definition KDP Print books are not returnable unless defective, but authors can decide on a return policy for books distributed from IngramSpark. The cost of returned books is deducted from the proceeds of your titles. What did you find out when you enquired? Does or will your local bookstore order books from KDP/Amazon? Not all bookstores will order books in the same way, but generally larger chains will have procedures in place that the store manager can't get around. I did my homework and my local (independent) bookstore orders from the Ingram list. What did you learn?

The last question is "What are your goals?" If you choose to focus, for example, on the sale of paperback books, that goal will result in you focusing on having your paperback available from IngramSpark for many of the reasons stated above. I can run through all the various scenarios, but ensure that the decisions you make will help you achieve your goals.

As a last thought for this chapter... I started this discussion saying there are many layers of strategies in publishing and selling books in this ever-changing world of book publishing. I've included quite a few articles in the Appendix of this book that will steer you in the direction of some ethical sources of information.

We're now going to cover a few bits and pieces that don't nicely fit into any other chapter and then finish out our discussion with the topic of companies that provide self-publishing assistance.

VIII

AUDIOBOOKS &
LOOSE ENDS

19

AUDIOBOOKS

A udiobooks have been sometimes difficult and often expensive to create for authors until recently. There are now two sources for us to create an audiobook: ACX and Findaway Voices. Although ACX has always been considered the primary creation point of audiobooks, competition is starting to appear —especially for non-US writers.

We'll start our discussion with ACX (http://acx.com) as it is still the primary creation point for audiobooks. A quote from their site:

> *ACX is a marketplace where authors, literary agents, publishers and other Rights Holders can connect with narrators, engineers, recording studios, and other Producers capable of producing a finished audiobook. ~ACX website*

ACX is an arm of Amazon and as you see from the quote above, they see themselves as a marketplace. ACX brings together the professionals involved in the creation of audiobooks with authors/publishers.

If you have already created an audio version of your book and just want to sell it, you can do that. If you are looking for a narrator, you can find one at ACX. Since ACX has a connection to Audible.com and Amazon.com and iTunes, once completed, every audiobook will be available on all these platforms.

I have created an audiobook on ACX and, although intimidating at first, I found that I was gently led through the various steps. These steps are:

1) **Rights** – The author confirms they own the audio rights for the book. If you are self-published and haven't signed a contract with a publisher, you own the rights.

2) **Profile** - Create a profile which contains information about the book —the title, a description of the book and a description of the type of narrator wanted. The profile also contains a 1-2 page excerpt from your book to serve as the audition script.

3) **Producer** - Once a profile is created the author can open the project up to auditions or listen to sample narrations and invite a select sample of producers/narrators to audition.

4) **Review auditions submitted** – If sample narrations are solicited, they can now be reviewed.

5) **Create a Deal** - Decide on the narrator that seems to suit the book the best and make an offer. Typically the project is paid for in two ways—outright payment to the narrator/producer on a "Per Finished Hour" basis, or a royalty split.

6) **Begin the project** - The chosen narrator will record a 15-minute sample and then wait for approval. Once approval is received, the whole project will be recorded and uploaded to the project dashboard.

7) **Approve the final product** - The author listens to the

entire project and requests corrections if necessary. Once approved, the narrator is paid unless a royalty split is in place.

8) **Distribute the audiobook** - An audiobook created at ACX will be automatically distributed to Audible, Amazon, and iTunes once the project is finalized.

9) **Promote** - Once an audiobook is available for sale, it is available to be added to your list of works to be promoted

10) **Earn Royalties** - The author earns royalties on each sale that is directly deposited to their bank account, just as royalties are deposited from e-book or paperback sales.

It sounds quite straightforward, doesn't it? In my experience, the hardest part of making an audiobook was choosing the narrator to record the audio. All the samples that I listened to were outstanding! The site has extensive help and FAQ documents that will lead every author through the process and answer any question that may come up. Authors are paid either 25% or 40% of retail sales, and the price of an audiobook is more than an e-book typically.

Findaway Voices can be seen as the new kid on the block. I first learned of them through a promotion via Draft2Digital. Findaway Voices is one part of a larger company that has fingers in many content pies. The parent company is not just involved in audiobooks, but dabbles in e-books, comics, apps and many other types of content. They joined forces with Draft2Digital in July 2017 and the plan is to produce and distribute audiobooks to over 170 retailers including the well-established ones— Amazon, Audible and iTunes.

Findaway Voices gives authors control of pricing, and

royalties are paid based on the list price. (ACX doesn't allow control over pricing.) The theory is that authors can attract new readers who might be willing to take a risk on an untried author, if the audiobook costs only a few dollars to purchase.

Findaway Voices has no geographic restrictions, and because of this, authors from any country can have an audiobook created.

The process seems similar to that of ACX. An account is created and details are provided about the book. A narrator is selected, the audio is recorded and then approved and published. They claim to have the largest distribution network, and by the list of partners they share, I'd agree.

The website (https://findawayvoices.com/authors-and-publishers/) even has a handy cost estimator.

Although I've not created an audiobook with this new company, it is on my list to try. I see it as yet another example of the world opening up to Indie Authors—especially non-American ones.

20

LOOSE ENDS

This chapter contains a selection of topics that don't fit anywhere else.

1) Look Inside and Free sample

Amazon offers two ways readers can have a sneak peak at a book before buying it. Look Inside is a way of looking at the content of a book without leaving the Amazon website. This functionality is attached to the Kindle version of all books on Amazon. To activate it, the reader needs to simply click on the cover and a popup window will appear with the first 10% of the book starting with the cover graphic. It is quite a sales vehicle. The book isn't just displayed plainly. Further information is displayed on either side of the text of the book. Details about the book, the rating, the price and a button to buy a copy can be found on the left side. The right side typically shows the reader's most recent viewing history. This whole package is popular with readers and an attractive sales vehicle for authors.

The last button on the Look Inside function is a "Try a

Sample" button. This brings us to the next functionality open to readers—the "Send a Free Sample to your Kindle" function. Instead of reading the first 10% of a book on a computer screen popup, readers can have a sample sent to their Kindle. Many prefer the reading environment of their Kindle or Kindle App. Once the reader gets to the end of the free sample, they are encouraged to purchase a copy.

2) Author Central

(https://authorcentral.amazon.com/gp/home)

Author Central is Amazon's author dashboard. Yes, I realize that Amazon has a whole bunch of arms and each has its own functionality, and yes, you do need to pay attention to this arm of Amazon. The Author Central comes into play after the first book is published and can be viewed as a master dashboard to view/add/edit the author's bio, identify which books belong to the author and view all reviews. Each geographical version of Amazon has its own Amazon Central—and they aren't yet attached. At this point four of them allow authors to add more information than just a bio. (There is an invitation-only beta at the time of the writing of this book that allows authors to access more than four Amazons) The extra information that is allowed varies from location to location. Amazon.com will allow the addition of an author's blog feed, author pictures and short videos. Amazon.co.uk, Amazon.de and Amazon.fr allow for a smaller selection of extra information.

In addition to adding extra information, authors can view a variety of ranking numbers from book rankings to author rankings.

I haven't had access to what Amazon is looking to roll out, but I'm assuming that it will allow easy addition of extra information to the central page. Once a book is published, it is to an author's advantage to set up as many Author Centrals as possible.

3) Amazon X-ray

Also called X-Ray for Authors is:

" a unique Kindle e-Book feature that allows readers to learn more about a character, topic, event, place, or any other term, simply by pressing and holding on the word or phrase that interests them." ~Amazon help docs

X-ray can be turned on for any Kindle book from the KDP Dashboard. Once activated and approved, the author will be able to edit the content that Amazon has pulled from various sources, notably Wikipedia. X-ray only applies to Kindle books and the idea behind this functionality is to enrich the reading experience. The author can add links to Wikipedia pages for what are called "terms" or words that can be defined and described. If the Wikipedia page doesn't work for the author's purposes, a custom definition or description can be created. A similar function exists for characters, but many see the character information as more informative as illustrated in the following quote:

"As a typical use case, Amazon cites the example of George R.R. Martin's "A Dance with Dragons," which has more than 400 characters. A reader encountering a character who was last mentioned 2,000 pages ago can tap on the X-Ray button in the app to get a quick rundown on the character's background and see excerpts from previous mentions."

https://www.geekwire.com/2012/amazon-kindle-brings-xray-iphone-ipad-app/

As a lover of Regency romances—books that often are written in series—I find I struggle to remember aspects of the world several books in. Having reference information right in the structure of the book is something I find very helpful!

IX

SELF-PUBLISHING
SERVICES

21

ABOUT SELF-PUBLISHING SERVICES

As you have determined in the preceding chapters, it is possible to self-publish a book all by yourself. As I said in one of the first chapters, it isn't overly difficult—in many cases just requiring some stubbornness. Many authors feel more comfortable hiring a company to help them with various aspects, or in fact decide that they want to turn the whole lot over to a company.

In this chapter we are going to talk about services or companies that work in the self-publishing world. Many of the most ethical services have an a la carte menu that allows authors to pick and choose services as well as a "we do everything for you" choice that allows for virtual hands off. What you choose is up to you. I will provide some starting points below and begin with the warning quote from the Alliance of Independent Authors.

"Starting out, many writers type 'self-publishing' into a Google search and instantly find themselves drowning in results, bogged down in jargon, or confused by who does what and who serves

whom. The answers to their questions are in there somewhere but framed in a hundred different ways by a thousand different people. Soon, instead of clarity, the writer emerges with a whole new suite of questions. How much should an editor cost? How do I protect my copyright? What is an ISBN? Do I need one? How do I get one? Is it worth paying for promotion?

...Tyro self-publishers can easily fall victim to literary fraud, scams, and misleading practices, duped by the pretense that their book is being 'published,' while in reality it is only being printed or formatted." ~ALLi

I find it personally heartbreaking to hear the stories of authors who have been taken advantage of. There are several well-known predators of authors who regularly have a table at publishing/writer's conferences and talk a good game. Many authors don't understand how badly they have been taken in until well after the fact. Many don't realize that they have bought a bunch of junk—much of it available for free.

There are well-known resources to tell the good guys from the mediocre guys from the bad ones. My go-to resource is: https://selfpublishingadvice.org/allis-self-publishing-service-directory/self-publishing-service-reviews/ The WatchDog desk of the Alliance of Independent Authors is thorough in their investigations and honest in their evaluations. Bookmark this page, as it is continually being updated and will serve as a great source of information for you going forward.

As we saw going through the various chapters of this book, all the parts and pieces can be done by the author themselves and/or by hiring various professionals. The key is to make an educated decision.

"The best assisted publishing companies are clear about what they are delivering and what you're paying for. The less than reputable companies you will receive countless emails and phone calls about 'must have services.'" ~ALLi

To continue on from the above quote, I believe that many authors end up being taken advantage of because they don't know the questions to ask. Let me start you off with a set of questions. Not all questions are applicable to all situations.

- If a contract has to be signed, have someone else review it with you or have a lawyer look it over. In many cases, dishonest companies trick you into agreeing to things you shouldn't have agreed to.

- Who holds the rights of your work (and what rights — paper, digital, etc.) and for how long? In self-publishing, typically you always hold your own rights.

- Is there an early termination fee for taking back your rights? This should be a red flag, but if you are comfortable signing away your rights, understand what would be involved in getting them back.

- What is the royalty split? In other words, how much is this service going to cost? Are they paid upfront or do they take a portion of the royalties?

- How often will you be paid? When dealing directly with retailers, you are paid once a month in general.

- Are there additional fees or charges? Do they charge for lowering the price of a book to put it on sale? Do they charge to fix typos?

- Do you have the ability to change the price to put your

book on sale? Some companies will actually refuse to change the price and as such the book can't be put on sale. This type of behavior should be seen as a red flag.

- Are there fees for service? What are they specifically? See the above point.

- Who owns the final book files? You should own your own book files and should be able to get source files for your records. This may entail a fee, however.

- Can you pick and choose your service provider—especially with respect to editors—or are you forced to use the company's editing staff? A potential red flag is being forced to use their staff regardless of skills or experience.

- Is there transparency of staff's skills and backgrounds? See above comment.

- Can you set the retail price? Unethical companies will try to steer authors towards a price that is outside of a normal range for their genre.

- Is there a clear breakdown of fees? As the saying goes— are you baffled by BS and don't really understand what the costs are?

- Where will your book be available for sale? Is there an available list of retailers?

- Are there odd charges? Such as fees for monthly accounting. Does the company seem to be padding their bill?

- How is the communication? Are they overly pushy?

Ask yourself: Where's the value? A self-publishing company may make things easier for authors by having access to editing, graphic design and formatting folks. But they also may charge a premium price for unnecessary services—pad the bill, as the saying goes.

An amorphous feature of many self-publishing services is the offer of marketing support. Self-publishing services may prey on the lack of knowledge of authors by offering things like press releases, which are generally not used by Indie Authors. Having a book listed on a company website that is not frequented by readers or listed in a catalogue that has a very small distribution is not helpful.

22

SELF-PUBLISHING SERVICES

As the quote from the beginning of the previous chapter stated, a quick Google search will return hundreds, if not thousands of companies ready and eager to take a beginning author's money.

For this section, I'll choose to highlight a few ethical, vetted services that can serve as a starting point in a search. Please make use of the vetting of ALLi's watchdog desk (https://selfpublishingadvice.org/allis-self-publishing-service-directory/self-publishing-service-reviews/) to ensure that any company you choose to hire will provide an honest return for your money.

Gatekeeper Press

Gatekeeper Press describes themselves as "a full-service publishing house and distribution aggregator who works with partners to produce and distribute high-quality books in digital and print formats." On their website they state a decade of experience.

Gatekeeper Press operates on a fee for service model so

the authors get 100% of royalties from the various platforms.

Although the emphasis seems to be on formatting and distribution, they offer a series of a la carte services such as cover design, editing and proofreading, illustrators and paperback printing. Both distribution and formatting are paid options—keep in mind distribution is free for many sources. For a list of their partners, see the list in the Appendix.

BookBaby

Book Baby has been in existence for a number of years and they offer a wide variety of packages and a la carte items. They either supply directly or via partners all aspects of publishing needs. My pet peeve with BookBaby is the fees for changes. They charge for content changes—be it correcting a typo that was overlooked or changing the front or back matter. If you use them for distribution, they will charge every time you want to change the price to put the book on sale. Although the various a la carte items seem to be priced at industry standards, the ~~cheap~~ frugal part of me gets my back up at being charged $25.00 to change the price of my book. It is, however, possible to use BookBaby's a la carte items and then directly upload files to Amazon, other retailers or aggregators yourself.

Matador Publishing

Matador has been offering self-publishing services since 1999 and is an arm of Troubador Publishing Ltd. located in the UK. Each book submission is evaluated individually and priced individually. They don't agree to work with all books submitted. They will determine what each project needs and will provide an estimate of costs. They are described as not particularly sales-y and extremely helpful with good customer service. Since they are an arm of Troubador Publishing, they have access to a level of distribution that isn't accessible to most self-published authors. In addition to the usual services, they have an a la carte list of various marketing services.

Page Master Publishing

Although Page Master Publishing seems to wear many hats, with regards to the book world, they describe themselves as a short-run publishing company. They can print anywhere from 2 to 5000 copies of your book. They offer a variety of services from editing, to formatting to cover design to printing to distribution. The website is a bit short on details of service staffs' experience and pricing for services rendered—quotes can be obtained by submitting a contact form. I include them here as they are a Canadian company based in Edmonton, AB.

Reedsy

Reedsy offers an interesting model to self-published authors. Their website states that they were founded in 2014 and have since helped authors produce over 3000 books. They have a different model than the above selection of self-publishing companies in that they connect authors with qualified service people. Authors create a free account and request quotes from registered service providers. Each service provider has a description page containing information about them and their work as well as some testimonials. Each service person can charge what they choose and it is up to the author to accept the quote they like the best. Reedsy has contacts for Editing, Design, Marketing, Publicity, Ghostwriting and Web Design. They don't offer a connection point to actually sell your book, however, and each service is paid for individually.

XinXii

XinXii describes themselves as Europe's leading e-Book Self-publishing and distribution platform. Authors can upload a wide variety of document types, and if uploading a Word document or similar file type, it can be formatted for free. To "pay" for the service, XinXii keeps a portion of the royalties. Authors keep roughly 85% of the royalties paid from the various retail sites. (In other words, they keep 15% of what is earned from the retailers.) Keep in mind that the primary retailers will pay royalties based on price point and possibly a few other factors like file size. For a list of their distribution partners see the Appendix.

As I mentioned at the beginning of this chapter, there are literally hundreds of service providers for self-publishing authors. This can be confirmed by doing a quick Google search. Although many are problematic, there are honest service providers out there. If hiring a service to help you manage your journey to being self-published, ask a lot of questions and don't hesitate to check ALLi's Watchdog list to vet your choices.

CONCLUSION

We've covered quite a bit in this book. So...are you done? No, not really. At this point you have enough information to put your book up for sale in e-book and print form on the major and minor retailers. You have some information on strategy to start you out. Now you have to start the process of promoting your book. I have lots of information on that in my other books. Remember, marketing is just like any other subject that you will face on your publishing journey —it is best learned one step at a time.

This publishing journey of yours has many layers of learning. The intent of this book is to be at a beginner level. I wanted to create a reference to get folks started on their publishing journey, a reference that would serve as a firm starting point. There are many nuances in publishing. Joining reliable writer's groups will help you on your publishing journey and help you find more reliable sources of information to guide you further. I maintain a website where I share up-to-date and accurate information about self-publishing with an emphasis on Canadian Self-publishing where I can find it. Feel free to subscribe to http://self-publishinginfo.com/ and receive updates in your inbox.

Thank you, as always, for choosing one of my books. Please take a few moments to share some thoughts about it on the retailer you purchased it from.

INTERESTED IN GETTING MORE TECHNICAL HELP?

Interested in getting some helpful hints and some helpful videos to your inbox. As I'm sure you are aware, authors are encouraged to give away free book to encourage people to join their mailing lists.

My books are different - they solve a problem. Just because you picked up one of my books doesn't mean you want a free book on a completely different topic. Because of this, I offer subscribers to my mailing list, free help - usually in the form of blog posts or YouTube Videos. I let everyone know about new releases and offer money off of my online courses.

If this sounds like something you would be interested in, join me at: http://bakerviewconsulting.com/reader-list/

X

APPENDIX

GLOSSARY

ACX - Audiobook Creation Exchange - an arm of Amazon that facilitates the creation and sale of an audiobook.

Agent-assisted self-publishing - this is a new type of self-publishing that has appeared in the last few years. In this situation, an agent who is unable to sell a book to a traditional publisher will help the author through the process of self-publishing and collect a portion of the royalties for their efforts.

Aggregators - is a service that takes your manuscript/finished file, converts it to the various digital formats needed for e-book distribution (if you don't upload final files) and delivers your book file to various retail outlets. Many Aggregators will have partnerships with retail outlets that self-published authors have difficulty accessing on their own.

Assisted self-publishing - refers to publishing with a team of experienced professionals to help with the process. This may be a company or a series of professionals. Also referred to as a Book Coach.

Collective publishing - this type of publishing often refers to a group working together, sharing skills to get all published. Similar to Joint Ventures, it is not unusual to see groups of authors with various skills collaborating and pooling these skills.

Custom graphics - graphics that are created from "scratch." This may mean general graphics or book covers and may be created from nothing or from stock photos and then manipulated using Adobe Photoshop or other similar program.

Distributers - the term that typically applies to a middleman used by traditional publishers to get paperback/hardcover books into bookstores.

Editing - the action of reviewing a manuscript and making changes of various sorts. Editing is carried out by the author as well as professional service providers.

Editor - a person with special training and experience to help revise and improve a manuscript or other piece of written material.

EPub - a file type created from a Word document that is accepted by all other sellers of electronic books except Amazon. This is a technology which is continually improving. EPubs that are created now are either ePub 2.0 or ePub 3.0.

Expanded Distribution - a term used by many retailers/aggregators to refer to a list of other partners they distribute books to beyond their own facility.

Flattened graphics - what starts out as a graphic that appears to have depth can be reduced in effect when it goes through the publishing process.

Going direct - means making choices all along the way that maximize your creative and commercial advantage, sourcing online tools and creative collaborators to supplement your own competencies and self-taught skills and getting stuck into hands-on book preparation and production. Learn by doing.

Gutter - the space on the inside of a paperback book between the inner edge of the text and the spine.

Hybrid publishing - refers to a type of partnership. This partnership is typically between an author and a small publishing company. If we assume that in traditional publishing the publisher pays for all costs of publishing and in indie/self-publishing the author pays for all costs, hybrid publishing is somewhere in the middle.

Hybrid author - So let's define a hybrid author as an author who is self-published or traditionally published depending on what suits the project or in fact parts of a project.

ISBN - (International Standard Book Number) is a 13-digit number that uniquely identifies each specific edition of a book or book-like product (an example of a book-like product can be an e-book). These 13 digits are divided into 5 parts. Each part is separated by a hyphen. They are:
1. The **EAN** (European article number) product code: the first three digits of the EAN barcode number

2. The **Group Identifier**: a single digit following the EAN product code that specifies the country or language in which the book is published

3. The **Publisher Prefix**: a number that identifies a particular publisher within the preceding group

4. The **Title Identifier**: a number that identifies a particular title or edition of a title issued by the preceding publisher

5. The **Check Digit**: a single digit at the end of the ISBN that validates the accuracy of the ISBN

Indie or independent publishing - often refers to a form of publishing that is done alone or without the support of a company or corporation to carry out many of the tasks. It can also refer to publishing that takes place outside of the old-school traditional realm.

Joint Ventures - a type of collaborative arrangement where authors play various roles, sometimes involving other service providers such as formatters. There are examples of groups of authors joining together to pool their resources and expertise to publish books of various descriptions—an example of this is multi-author box sets.

KDP - Kindle Direct Publishing. This is the arm of Amazon that is primarily responsible for publishing electronic or Kindle versions of books. Recently, they have started to branch out into creating and publishing print versions also.

KDP Select - an exclusive arrangement with Kindle Direct Publishing that lasts for three months at a time. While a book is "in" KDP Select the electronic version of it can't be available anywhere else.

KENP - Kindle Edition Normalized Pages. This number determines the royalties authors earn from KU and KOLL.

Kindle Countdown Deal - a KDP Select benefit that lets authors run limited-time discount promotions for their books that are available on Amazon.com and Amazon.co.uk. Customers will see both the regular price and the promotional price on the book's detail page, as well as a countdown clock showing how much time is left at the promotional price.

Kindle Create - a new service from Amazon that will take a Word document (or similar) and convert it to a Kindle book and upload it directly to Amazon for publishing through the KDP dashboard.

KOLL - Kindle Owner's Lending Library. Amazon Prime members can read one book each month as part of their membership.

KU - Kindle Unlimited. This is a subscription service available to US, Canada and UK folks who pay one fee per month and can read unlimited books that are enrolled in KDP Select.

Legacy publishing - a term used to refer to what many call Traditional Publishing. It is used often to indicate that the big traditional publishers are considered to be old-school by many, dinosaurs by many and gradually disappearing from the marketplace.

Margins - the space between the edge of text and the edge of a page for a paperback book.

Mobi - the file type which serves as the precursor to Amazon's Kindle book. Generally created from a Word document.

Multilayered graphics for cover graphics - many graphic artists are skilled at creating graphics that appear to have depth. This is done through the process of creating multiple overlaid graphics using Adobe Photoshop or another program. This effect is typically "flattened" by the publishing process, especially when referring to POD publishing.

Partnership publishing - like hybrid publishing, partnership publishing refers to some sort of agreement or partnership between the author and various service providers.

Paypal - a payment processor that allows invoices to be issued, money to be sent or collected in a wide variety of currencies.

Payoneer - a payment processor that claims to serve over 200 countries, in 150 currencies in 35 languages with 4M account holders.

PDF - stands for Portable Document Format. It is the file format that is used to create print books. The text is considered to be static or frozen on a PDF document.

Premade covers - book covers that are mostly created around a theme or subject matter. The graphic designer just needs to add the book title and author information and it is ready for use.

Resolution - the measure of the sharpness of an image usually expressed in the density of pixels per square inch or dpi.

Retail platform - a place (for the sake of this book) that will sell your book in some form to a reader.

Self-publishing - this phrase refers to publishing that is directed by the author, but the tasks are not always literally done by the author.

Serif fonts vs non-serif fonts - serif fonts have little feet, little flourishes. An example is Times New Roman. Non-serif fonts are smooth and without embellishments. An example is Arial.

Shared publishing - similar to Joint Ventures, this term indicates shared responsibility amongst a group of people.

Stock photos - photos or other graphics that are purchased from commercial sites. These photos may or may not have rules governing their use.

Subsidized publishing - this is a term that often applies to projects that are funded by organizations. Often anthologies or poetry collections that are organized and published by writer's groups have the costs paid for by the organization, not the authors' themselves.

Thumbnail graphic - a small-size graphic typically in the range of 150px X 150px. Can be square or rectangular in shape.

Traditional publishing - the author pays nothing and receives royalties and perhaps an advance. The publisher is responsible for editing, cover graphics, formatting, and distribution.

Trim size - the outside measurement of the size of a book. Expressed in W x H in inches.

Vanity publishing - many authors who, for one reason or another, decided to not go the traditional publishing route, found a way to publish their own books. Frequently this involved finding a printer to print copies of paperbacks and either selling them on a personal website or on a consignment basis at a neighborhood bookstore.

CHART OF DISTRIBUTORS

Smashwords
- B&N
- Apple/iBook
- Scrib'd
- Overdrive
- Tolino
- Odilo
- WH Smith
- Gardners
- Yuzu
- Inktera
- FNAC
- Askews & Holts Library
- Baker & Taylor
- Livraria Cultura
- Browns Books for Students
- Hive.co.uk
- Axis 360
- Blio

Ingram Print
US & Canada
•Amazon
•Barnes & Noble
•Chapters (Indigo)
UK/Europe
•Alibris
•Agapea
•Amazon.co.uk
•Aphrohead
•Bertrams
•Book Depository Ltd
•Books Express
•Coutts Information Services Ltd
•Designarta Books
•Eden Interactive Ltd
•Foyles
•Gardners
•Trust Media Distribution
•Mallory International
•Paperback Shop Ltd.
•Superbookdeals
•The Book Community Ltd
•Waterstones
•Wrap Distribution
Australia & New Zealand
•Booktopia
•Fishpond
•The Nile
•James Bennett
•ALS
•Peter Pal
•University Co-operative Bookshop

Ingram Online Retail

- 24Symbols
- 7Switch
- Amazon
- Apple
- Baker & Taylor Blio
- Barnes & Noble
- BookShout (Rethink Books)
- Bookmate
- EBSCO
- Follett
- Gardners
- Glose
- Hummingbird DM
- Inktera
- Kobo
- PaperC
- Redshelf
- Rockstand (RockASAP)
- Sainsbury
- Txtr
- Wook
- Zola
- A Book Company
- All Romance e-Books
- Artech House
- Asia Books
- BOL.com
- Bookshop Krisostomus
- Booktopia
- Campus e-Books
- Cokesbury.com
- Completebook.com
- Covenant
- DMC
- Ebook.de Internet GmbH

- e-BookMall
- e-BookShop
- FeedBooks
- Five Senses Education Pty Ltd
- Global Reward Systems
- Hastings
- Infibeam
- Inkterra
- Iwemi.com
- KIOWPPE
- Julke Entertainment GmbH
- Libstor
- Sybrary.com
- Majesty Media Group
- Mediander, LLC
- Mintbook.com
- MPH Online
- My Learning Hub
- Online Book Place
- Pocketbook
- PubFront APS
- Saraiva e Siciliano
- Sarajoben Enterprises US
- SBS Special Book Services
- Slicebooks
- Spotlink Digital
- Takealot
- Textbooks.comMBS
- Tradebit
- UAB VIPSupply
- Wisepress LTD UK
- XAMOnline

Draft2Digital
- Amazon

- iBooks
- Barnes & Noble
- Kobo
- Inktera
- Playster
- Scrib'd
- Tolino
- 24Symbols
- OverDrive

Gatekeepers

1. iBookstore
2. Amazon
3. Barnes & Noble
4. Blio
5. CoreSource
6. Follett
7. Freading
8. Gardners Books
9. Google Play
10. Kobo
11. Overdrive
12. Scrib'd
13. Wheelers Books
14. Baker & Taylor
15. Ingram
16. Nacscorp

PublishDrive

- iBookstore
- Google Play Books
- Amazon
- Kobo
- Overdrive
- Scrib'd

- •Playster
- •Barnes & Noble
- •CNPeReading
- •Bookmate
- •Tolino
- •Odilo
- •Ipubs
- •BookShout!
- •Gardners.com
- •E-sentral
- •Ciando
- •Tookbook
- •Libri
- •Mackin
- •24Symbols
- •Casadellibro
- •Redshelf
- •Rockstand
- •Ekonyv
- •Bookline
- •Lira
- •Multimediaplaza
- - DangDang
- •E-letoltes

Kobo

- •Angus & Robertson (Australia)
- •Bookworld (Australia)
- •Collins (Australia)
- •Livraria Cultura (Brazil)
- •Indigo (Canada)
- •FNAC (France)
- •PriceMinister (India)
- •WH Smith (Ireland)
- •Eason & Son Ltd. (Italy)

- Feltrinelli (Italy)
- Mondadori (Japan)
- Rakuten (Netherlands)
- Bol (New Zealand)
- The Paper Plus Group (Philippines)
- National Book Store (Portugal)
- FNAC (Spain)
- La Central (UK)
- American Booksellers Association (Participating Stores)

XinXii

- Amazon
- Angus & Robertson
- Buchide
- Buecher.de
- Casa Del Libro
- Family Christian
- FNAC
- GooglePlay
- Hugendubel
- IBookstore/iTunes
- Indigo
- Kobo
- Libris BLZ
- Livaria Cultura
- Mondadori
- B&N
- Rakuten
- Scrib'd
- Thalia
- Weltbild
- Whitcoulls
- WHSmith

FILE REQUIREMENTS

Amazon
KDP (Kindle Direct Publishing- for electronic version of a book)- will accept .doc, .docx, HTML, mobi, ePub, RTF, Plain Text, KPF (now has Kindle Create)

KDP Print (for the print copy of a book) - PDF

Kobo - will accept ePub, .doc, .docx, .mobi, .odt

Barnes & Noble - .doc, .docx, .txt, .rtf, .htm, .html, .epub

iTunes - epub 2.0.1 or later

Draft 2 Digital - .doc, .docx, .rtf, .ePub

Ingram - print - PDF/X-1a:2001 or PDF/X-3:2002 (created from Acrobat or Indesign) with the file name of isbn_txt.pdf or isbntxt.pdf
Ingram e-Book - EPUB 3.0 (can't accept enhanced EPUB

3.0 files) with front cover RGB and a minimum of 600px along longest axis

Cover Requirements

E-book cover
Height/width ratio of 1:1.6 (for Amazon/KDP) or 1:1.5 (for most other retailers)
File type - jpeg/jpg or tif/tiff
Required size - 1600px X 2560px (for Amazon) or 1600 X 2400 (all other retailers)
File Size & resolution - must be less than 50MB and a resolution of 72dpi
Color - products display on the website using RGB color mode (do not use CMYK or sRBG)
Borders - cover art with a white background or very light backgrounds seem to disappear against the white background of many retail sites. Consider adding a narrow border to define the edges of the cover graphic.

Paperback cover

Height/width are determined according to the page count, trim size and paper choice. KDP Print and IngramSpark have templates that can be downloaded to help with sizing. (https://kdp.amazon.com/en_US/cover-templates) (https://myaccount.ingramspark.com/Portal/Tools/CoverTemplateGenerator)

File type - PDF only

Content - the title, subtitle, author name and series information on the cover must match the information entered in the book record and must be legible. KDP Print will kick out covers that contain a mismatch between cover content and book details.

Spine text can only be used if the paperback has a minimum of 100 pages.

Resolution - the finished product must have a minimum resolution of 300 dpi. Even if the graphic used to create the PDF has multiple layers, it will all be flattened to one layer. For more information on multiple layer graphics and resolution, see the appendix.

List of possible trim sizes from KDP Print.
Full-color interior books:
5.5" x 8.5"
6" x 9"
6.14" x 9.21"
7" x 10"
8" x 10"
8.5" x 8.5"
8.5" x 11"

Black and white interior books:
5" x 8"
5.06 x 7.81"
5.25" x 8"
5.5" x 8.5"
6" x 9"

6.14" x 9.21"
6.69" x 9.61"
7" x 10"
7.44" x 9.69"
7.5" x 9.25"
8" x 10"
8.5" x 11"

WHAT DO EDITORS DO?

Adaptations
Adapting content (Usually includes substantive and structural editing)

Canadianization
Editing American or British text to make it conform to Canadian spelling and usage.

Consultation for academic writers
Preliminary or developmental discussion about an academic thesis or research project.

Copy editing
Editing for grammar, spelling, punctuation and other mechanics of style.

Correspondence: government
Writing letters on behalf of ministers and other government officials.

Cross-language editing/proofreading

Comparative editing/proofreading of the same material in two or more languages for consistency and accuracy. May include Canadianization of English-language materials or Americanization of British or Canadian materials.

Developmental editing

Developing or helping to develop a project from proposal and rough manuscript to final manuscript or final product, incorporating input from author(s) and others. May include scheduling, costing/budgeting, supervising design and coordinating production.

Desktop publishing/document design

Layout and typesetting. May include selecting graphics.

Electronic forms

Creating forms to be filled out electronically using fields, drop-down menus and check-boxes.

Fact/reference checking
Checking the accuracy of facts and/or quotes by referring to the author's original sources or other sources.

Gender and bias editing

Editing to avoid bias in matters of gender and ethnicity. May be done during copy and stylistic editing, or may be a separate function.

Grant proposal writing

Consulting on or helping to prepare applications for grant funding.

Indexing

Producing an alphabetical list of names and subjects that appear in a work, including the page references.

Manuscript evaluation
Assessing manuscripts, including book-length fiction and non-fiction works, for publication. Includes evaluating for content, structure and style, and estimating the possible market potential of the work.

Mock-up (rough paste-up) Producing a mock-up from proofs and marking the proofs for changes; inserting the page numbers in the table of contents and cross-references if necessary. May include copy fitting and/or marking color breaks.

Online editing Receiving manuscripts in electronic form and editing on-screen, using tracking software if required. See also specific types of editing, and Website/page evaluation, editing and writing.

Picture research
Locating suitable visuals, e.g., photographs, reproductions and illustrations. May include negotiating reprint permissions, copyright agreements and royalties.

Plain language editing
Simplifying language and style and eliminating jargon in order to make text easier to understand. Similar to Stylistic editing in intent, but often involves more rewriting/reworking. May include changing or unifying the reading level.

Proceedings
Recording and transcribing proceedings of conferences and similar events.

Production/pre-press/print coordination
Coordinating single- or multi-media projects. May include sourcing, costing, scheduling, and supervising design, photography/visuals, pre-press, print, bindery and distribution.

Project management
Managing a project from inception to final manuscript or final product, incorporating the work of writers, designers, desktop publishers, and other specialists. May include budgeting, scheduling, hiring, supervising design, estimating print costs and coordinating production.

Proofreading
Checking edited proofs for errors and omissions. May include incorporating or checking incorporation of author's alterations and cross-checking table of contents to page numbers, indices or appendices.

Research
Gathering information to support new or existing bodies of work.

Rewriting
Creating a new manuscript or parts of a manuscript based on existing text. Generally involves additional research and writing new material.

Stylistic editing
Clarifying meaning, eliminating jargon and improving the flow of language and ideas. May include checking or correcting the reading level, creating or recasting tables and/or figures, and negotiating changes with the author.

Substantive and structural editing
Clarifying and/or reorganizing a manuscript for content and structure. May include some rewriting, with author's agreement.

Technical editing
Editing technical texts to ensure that terms are used appropriately and that the language is readable and accurately conveys the author's meaning. May include editing scientific materials, and editing to a research journal style.

Template design
Designing a skeleton or master layout to provide consistency for a suite of documents.

Transcription/preparing texts
Transcribing and editing taped interviews. May be similar to Proceedings.

Translation
Rendering a manuscript in another language.

Website/page evaluation, editing and writing
Evaluating and/or editing new or existing Web pages or sites for coherence, content, language and usage, length and links. May also include writing new material.

Website/page design
Designing and/or creating new sites or pages for the Internet. May include work on site architecture, content, hypertext links, electronic forms and templates, etc.

Writing
Creating a new work based on research done by the editor/writer. May include editing.

BIBLIOGRAPHY

Web Articles

Author Earnings
http://authorearnings.com/report/october-2016/
http://authorearnings.com/report/dbw2017/
http://authorearnings.com/report/february-2017/
http://authorearnings.com/report/january-2018-report-us-online-book-sales-q2-q4-2017/

Britannica
https://www.britannica.com/topic/Amazoncom

Geekwire
https://www.geekwire.com/2012/amazon-kindle-brings-xray-iphone-ipad-app/

Lulu
http://www.lulu.com/blog/2010/03/the-importance-of-editing/#sthash.Fsl8XlfA.dpbs

PEAVI
http://peavi.ca/hire-an-editor/what-do-editors-do/

Smashwords
https://www.smashwords.com/list

The Book Designer
https://www.thebookdesigner.com/2013/08/book-layouts-page-margins/
https://www.thebookdesigner.com/2010/09/3-keys-to-beautiful-book-pages/

Vellum
http://blog.180g.co/2014/01/why-ebooks/

Webpedia
https://www.webopedia.com/TERM/I/ibooks.html

Chuck Wendig
http://terribleminds.com/ramble/2013/04/23/what-the-hell-is-a-hybrid-author-anyway/

Books
Successful Self-Publishing by Joanna Penn

Choosing the Best Self-Publishing Companies & Services 2018 by Jim Giammateo and John Dopler

RESOURCES

Retailer/Aggregator resources

KDP Print:
How to Create an Interior PDF of Your Book:
https://kdp.amazon.com/en_US/help/topic/G200645680

Cover creator

https://kdp.amazon.com/en_US/help/topic/G201953020

KDP (Kindle Direct Publishing)) Help
https://kdp.amazon.com/en_US/help?ref_=TN_help

Kobo Resources:

FAQ -
http://download.kobobooks.com/writinglife/Kobo/en-US/KWL_FAQ.pdf
User Guide:

http://download.kobobooks.com/writinglife/Kobo/en-US/KWL-User-Guide.pdf

iTunes/iBook Resources:

Support - https://support.apple.com/en-ca/HT201478

Publisher User Guide - https://itunesconnect.apple.com/docs/iTunesConnect_PublisherUserGuide.pdf

Draft2Digital Resources:

FAQ: https://draft2digital.com/faq/

Smashwords:

FAQ: https://www.smashwords.com/about/supportfaq

IngramSpark help:

IngramSpark cover creator tool - http://bit.ly/2FxEhZH

IngramSpark Pocket Guide to Publishing - http://bit.ly/2p8dmgb

ACX Resources

https://audible-acx.custhelp.com/

Ereader and App Help

AmazonCA Device Support: http://amzn.to/2tC4JQr

Kobo Help:

Kobo reader help: https://www.kobo.com/help/?style=onestore&store=CA&language=en-CA&culture=en-CA

Calibre: https://calibre-ebook.com/

BISAC Codes

http://bisg.org/page/BISACSubjectCodes

ISBNs
International ISBN Agency
https://www.isbn-international.org/

ISBN – Library & Archives Canada
https://www.bac-lac.gc.ca/eng/services/isbn-canada/Pages/create-account-isbn-canada.aspx

Bowker's PDF
https://bowker-apps.s3.amazonaws.com/myid50/s3fs-public/sites/default/files/images/Title_setup_and_registration.pdf

Bowker's ISBN Guides: Basic Information
https://bowker-apps.s3.amazonaws.com/myid50/s3fs-public/sites/default/files/images/MYID%2BBasic%2bInformation.pdf

US Copyright information
https://www.copyright.gov/

Nielson FAQ PDF
http://www.isbn.nielsenbook.co.uk/uploads/Independent%20Publisher%20Brochure%202017_Digital(2).pdf

Graphic Designers

Michelle Fairbanks – Fresh Design – Vancouver Island
https://mfairbanks.carbonmade.com/

Jess at Audiobookworm Promotions
https://audiobookwormpromotions.com/

Eva Ruutopold
http://ruu2.com/

Other Graphic Designers
Ebook Launch - http://ebooklaunch.com/ebook-cover-design/ prices range from $99 to $279
Laura Shinn - http://laurashinn.yolasite.com/my-cover-designs.php
PreMade Covers 4 U - http://www.premadecovers4u.com/
Your Ebook Cover - http://www.yourebookcover.com/portfolio.html
Jeremy Taylor - https://www.jeremytaylor.eu/books/e-book-cover-designs-introduction/
Custom ebook covers - http://www.customebookcovers.com/
Caligraphics - https://caligraphics.net/index.php
Cover Counts - http://www.thecovercounts.com/
The Miss Mae Site - http://www.themissmaesite.com/p/designing-book-covers.html
Mother Spider - http://motherspider.com/digital-book-cover/
Vila Design - https://www.viladesign.net/
Fiona Jayde Media - http://fionajaydemedia.com/
Covers by Ramona - http://coversbyramona.blogspot.ca/
Book Covers - http://bookcovers.us/
Hadleigh Design - http://www.hadleighdesign.com/

Self Pub Book Covers -
https://www.selfpubbookcovers.com/
Brett Grimes - http://www.brettgrimes.com/
Mark's list of low cost resources -
https://www.smashwords.com/list

Upworks (http://upworks.com) freelancers for hire
Reedsy (http://reedsy.com) freelancers for hire

Stock Photo sites:

Bigstockphoto.com
Shutterstock.com
https://www.istockphoto.com/ca

ARTICLES FOR FURTHER READING

Information on DRM

DRM Definition: https://techterms.com/definition/drm
What is Kindle DRM?: https://itstillworks.com/kindle-drm-17841.html
Amazon help thread on DRM:
https://kdp.amazon.com/community/thread.jspa?
threadID=157348

Articles on book design

Book Design: The Architecture:
https://www.thebookdesigner.com/2016/02/book-page-architecture/
How to Design Running Heads for Your Book:
https://www.thebookdesigner.com/2014/03/how-to-design-running-heads-for-your-book/
Understanding Book Layouts and Page Margins:
https://www.thebookdesigner.com/2013/08/book-layouts-page-margins/

3 keys to Beautiful Book Pages:
https://www.thebookdesigner.com/2010/09/3-keys-to-beautiful-book-pages/
21 Top Links to Book Fonts for Self-Publishing:
https://www.thebookdesigner.com/2012/07/top-font-links/
Picking Fonts for Your Self-Published Book:
https://www.thebookdesigner.com/2012/06/picking-fonts-for-your-self-published-book/

Articles on KDP Select

The Pros and Cons of Exclusivity :
https://www.thecreativepenn.com/2014/08/30/exclusivity/
Amazon KDP Select: Is It Worthwhile to Authors? :
https://www.janefriedman.com/amazon-kdp-select/
Don't Limit Your Book Distribution: CreateSpace, KDP Select, and ACX:
http://www.ingramspark.com/blog/amazon-exclusive-options-createspace-kdp-select-and-acx
KDP Rules Roundup: https://selfpublishingadvice.org/kdp-rules-roundup/

Articles from ALLi

Self-publishing services reviewed and rated:
https://selfpublishingadvice.org/allis-self-publishing-service-directory/self-publishing-service-reviews/

Articles from Author Earnings

Print vs Digital, Traditional vs Non-Traditional, Book-store vs Online:
http://authorearnings.com/report/dbw2017/

Oct 2016 Author Earnings Report: A Turning of the Tide: http://authorearnings.com/report/october-2016/
February 2017 Big Bad Wide & International Report: http://authorearnings.com/report/february-2017/

Articles on formatting from Word / YouTube videos

Complete Book Formatting How to Guide for Word Templates: https://www.youtube.com/watch?v=sH0Xoo_PYWw&t=792s
How to format a book in Microsoft Word (2017): https://www.youtube.com/watch?v=WdRKDq9tbRM
Adobe Indesign Book Template Walkthrough: https://www.youtube.com/watch?v=NpA5cZK8B7k

Articles on Keywords and Categories

Amazon: https://kdp.amazon.com/en_US/help/topic/G200652170
IngramSpark: http://www.ingramspark.com/blog/the-basics-of-book-metadata-and-keywords
How to Choose the Best Keywords when Publishing Fiction on Amazon: https://selfpublishingadvice.org/how-to-choose-the-best-keywords-when-publishing-on-amazon/
The Importance of Keywords to Rank Your Book on Amazon: https://www.thebookdesigner.com/2016/02/importance-of-keywords-to-ranking-your-book-on-amazon/

Cover design

99 Designs -How to design a book cover: the ultimate guide https://99designs.ca/blog/tips/book-cover-design/
Book Cover Design from The Creative Penn https://www.thecreativepenn.com/bookcoverdesign/

Goins Writer - Book Cover Design:
https://goinswriter.com/book-cover-design/
Reedsy - Book Cover Design: How self-published authors
can do it best https://blog.reedsy.com/book-cover-design/

Guidance for Blurbs:

Best Page Foreward - http://www.bestpageforward.net/
The Creative Penn -
https://www.thecreativepenn.com/2010/11/16/how-to-
write-back-blurb-for-your-book/
Kindlepreneur - https://kindlepreneur.com/back-book-
cover-blurb/
Self Publishing Advice -
https://selfpublishingadvice.org/how-to-write-a-blurb-for-
a-self-published-book/

Bookstores
Huff Post article about bookstores not carrying books with
CreateSpace ISBN
https://www.huffingtonpost.com/brooke-warner/5-
reasons-why-your-book-i_b_6934314.html

YOUTUBE VIDEOS

Bakerview Consulting videos

Vellum - https://www.youtube.com/watch?v=M2h7usWlHhg
Load a book to a Kindle App -
https://www.youtube.com/watch?v=VPhfHawMn4A&t=5s

Videos recommended by Jutoh

https://www.youtube.com/watch?v=g3lvhRpJrIg
https://www.youtube.com/watch?v=SWL0XIXD2r0

John Griffin - Jutoh instructional videos

https://www.youtube.com/watch?time_continue=13&v=TWQRZj7l0Ng
https://www.youtube.com/watch?time_continue=6&v=3BWPT-zwFN0
https://www.youtube.com/watch?time_continue=5&v=ZPItILMdgmY

https://www.youtube.com/watch?v=DBWdl-WcFTg

Scrivener videos and courses

Gwen Hernandez - https://scrivenerclasses.com/
Compiling video - https://www.youtube.com/watch?
v=rUkdHuC57Xc

Sigil video

https://www.youtube.com/watch?
v=HFsGemVlnYk&list=PL5hp8dDVPHGBJiBNh0T2YMln
B8r7lOOy2

Joel Friedlander's YouTube channel

https://www.youtube.com/user/jfbookman

Kindle Create

https://www.youtube.com/watch?
v=Y0LnxdqdlHI&list=PLE1Y2pbwRpkgh9fe4P8hKGJ55s2x
4oZz7&index=12

KDP University

https://www.youtube.com/watch?
v=BpqR4Worjjo&list=PLE1Y2pbwRpkgh9fe4P8hKGJ55s2x
4oZz7

WRITERS GROUPS

Professional Writer's Association of Canada
https://www.pwac.ca/

The Writer's Union of Canada
https://www.writersunion.ca/

Canadian Authors https://canadianauthors.org/national/

Canadian Literature Center http://www.abclc.ca

Writer's Trust of Canada
http://www.writerstrust.com/About.aspx

PEN Canada http://pencanada.ca/

Asian Canadian Writer's Workshop
http://www.asiancanadianwriters.ca/

InScribe Christian Writers' Fellowship https://inscribe.org/

Crime Writers of Canada
http://www.crimewriterscanada.com/

Writer's Guild of Canada
http://www.writersguildofcanada.com/

Science Writers & Communicators of Canada
http://sciencewriters.ca/

Federation of BC Writers http://www.bcwriters.ca/

Quebec Writers' Federation http://www.qwf.org/

The Word Guild https://thewordguild.com/

Writers & Editors Network http://wenetwork.ca/site/

Writers' Federation of New Brunswick https://wfnb.ca/

Young Writers of Canada
https://youngwritersofcanada.ca/

Writers Guild of Canada
http://www.wgc.ca/resources/agents.html

Writer's Federation of Nova Scotia http://writers.ns.ca/

Prince Edward Island Writers' Guild
https://www.peiwritersguild.com/

Writer's Collective of Manitoba
http://www.thewriterscollective.org/

Horror Writing Association http://horror.org/

Science Fiction and Fantasy Writers Association of America
http://www.sfwa.org/

Society of Children's Book Writers and Illustrators
https://www.scbwi.org/

The Author's Guild https://www.authorsguild.org/

American Society of Journalists and Authors
https://asja.org/

Romance Writers of America https://www.rwa.org/

The National Writers Union https://nwu.org/

National Association of Writers' Groups
http://www.nawg.co.uk/

The International Women's Guild https://www.iwwg.org/

Pacific Northwest Writer's Association PNWA.org

Pan African Writers Association
http://www.panafricanwritersassociation.org/

Historical Writers' Association
https://historicalwriters.org/

Horror Writers Association's UK http://hwauk.org/

The New Zealand Society of Authors
https://authors.org.nz/writers-organisations/

Australian Crime Writers Association
https://www.austcrimewriters.com/

The DC Science Writers Association https://dcswa.org/

Historical Writers of America
http://historicalwritersofamerica.org/

SOURCES OF EDITORS

ALLi partner services
https://www.allianceindependentauthors.org/services-directory/

Editors Canada:
http://editors.ca

Professional Editor Association of Vancouver Island:
peavi.ca/

Society for Editors and Proofreaders
https://www.sfep.org.uk/

Editorial Freelancers Association
https://www.the-efa.org/

ACES The Society for Editing
https://aceseditors.org/

National Association of Independent Writers and Editors
https://naiwe.com/

ABOUT THE AUTHOR

Social Media and WordPress Consultant Barb Drozdowich has taught in colleges, universities and in the banking industry. More recently, she brings her 15+ years of teaching experience and a deep love of books to help authors develop the social media platform needed to succeed in today's fast evolving publishing world. She delights in taking technical subjects and making them understandable by the average person. She owns Bakerview Consulting and manages the popular blog, Sugarbeat's Books, where she talks about Romance novels.

She is the author of 17 books, over 50+ YouTube videos, an online Goodreads course, a MailChimp/Mailerlite online course and an online WordPress course, all focused on helping authors and bloggers. Barb lives in the mountains of British Columbia with her family.

Barb can be found on her Book Blog, Business Blog, Pinterest, Google+, Goodreads, and Youtube

As well as:
barbdrozdowich.com
barb@bakerviewconsulting.com

ALSO BY BARB DROZDOWICH

All my books start with a problem that needs a solution - with a group of authors letting me know about a subject that they don't understand. I take it, break it down and see if I can add some clarity.

The books I've written attack the subjects of:

1) Understanding the world of Book Bloggers and Book Reviewers

2) Understanding all the parts and pieces of an author's online presence at a beginner's level

3) Understand the world of book promotions

4) Understanding What to blog, How to blog and Why to blog for authors

5) Understand how to use Goodreads as a tool of networking and communication with readers

6) Understand mailing lists and newsletters

7) Understand how to self-publish a book

During a recent workshop I gave on self-publishing, I walked participants through an exercise to help them understand the power of e-readers as well as the limits of e-readers. I was talking about the fact that not all e-readers can make use of clickable links as not all are connected to the internet or have browser capabilities. We also talked about creating links that readers from a variety of countries can actually use - my example was around solely using an Amazon.com link. Suddenly the light went in my own head about all of the clickable links I put in my books. So... going forward I'm directing everyone to a page that contains information about all of my books and buy links that are associated with those books. The link is easy to type in manually

or click on if you have the ability. It is:
https://readerlinks.com/mybooks/733

Below find a short description of each of my books and don't
hesitate to use the link above to find out more information in
terms of formats available and places to purchase a copy.

The Authors Guide to Working with Book Bloggers

This book is the first book I wrote and is centered around
information I received in a survey of book bloggers. This
information has been updated through a second, more extensive
survey. It is meant to serve as a primer for authors just entering
the world of book bloggers or book reviewers. It helps explain the
world of reviewers so that authors can walk confidently into that
world and get some attention for a book.

More information: https://readerlinks.com/mybooks/733

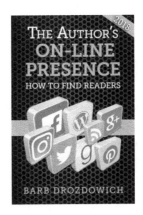

The Author's On-Line Presence: How to find readers

This book attacks the subject of "what is an author's on-line presence?" Whether we use the word 'presence' or 'platform,' many beginner authors are intimidated by all the information swirling about the internet. The list of "must do" seems totally overwhelming. This book breaks down this subject into easy to understand chucks in normal language.

More information: https://readerlinks.com/mybooks/733

The Author's Guide to Book Promotions

This book was also borne out of many discussions with authors. What is a book blog tour? What is a promotional newsletter? How do I determine which promotion company to use? I break down the language and explain this world in easy to understand English. This book also has large lists of book tour companies as well as book promotion companies which will help you start your search.

More information: https://readerlinks.com/mybooks/733

Blogging for Authors

Blogging is not dead as far as I'm concerned. It is alive and kicking! Blogging can be a very powerful way to communicate with readers. This book explains all aspects of blogging from what to say, to what platform to use, to how much it is going to cost.

More information: https://readerlinks.com/mybooks/733

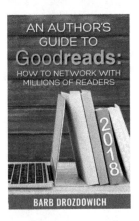

An Author's Guide to Goodreads: How to Network with Millions of Readers

Goodreads seems to the site with so much power yet creates so much frustration in authors. I often describe this site as a rabbit's warren because of how difficult it is to navigate. This book will walk you through all aspects of how to effectively use Goodreads to communicate with readers. It also has a **Free course**

More information: https://readerlinks.com/mybooks/733

Top Advice for Authors Promoting Their Book and Book Blogger Survey

As I've mentioned previously, I've carried out several surveys of bloggers and written about the results. My first book, The Author's Guide to Working with Book Bloggers is the first book based on survey results. The two books pictured above are also based on survey results. The first one is simply the unfiltered collection of answers to the question: "If you could give an author one piece of advice about promoting their book, what would it be?" This book lists all 500+ responses. The second book is a full analysis of all 30+ questions. If you are interested in finding out real information about the book blogging/book reviewer world, these books will help.

More information: https://readerlinks.com/mybooks/733

The Complete Mailing List Toolkit

I like to say that this book covers mailing lists and newsletters from soup to nuts. It doesn't focus on one aspect of communicating with readers, it covers it all. Each section is available individually and this book also has a free course associated with it.

More information: https://readerlinks.com/mybooks/733

What is Blogging?

AT ITS HEART, blogging is just another form of communication. In my mind there isn't a lot of difference between blogging and having a chat with some friends over a cup of coffee. You'll notice that I'm using the words "chat" or "conversation." When we're talking about blogging, I want you to keep the word "dialogue" in mind.

A blog is neither a billboard, nor a monologue. Blogging should be a dialogue.

Although I refer to the words "conversation" and "dialogue," your first response may be that no one talks on your blog, or that no one leaves comments for you to respond to. Times have changed.

The face of a conversation has changed in the electronic world. The person with whom we are chatting may not literally respond with words – they might respond with actions such as sharing your post with their friends on Facebook. They are doing the electronic equivalent of "Come over here and listen to this person." The electronic version is more along the lines of "This is great information; please go and read it." That's a response and in the big picture, that's a much more important response. Although I'm the first one to admit that comments are wonderful, such interaction is between two people. I have 16,000+ followers on Twitter. If I share on Twitter, it's pretty likely that more people than just myself will be part of the conversation. It's also pretty likely that a handful of my 16,000+ followers will join in, in their own way.

If you have a WordPress blog, one of the people you are "speaking" to might click on the Like button or in fact be so moved by what you have to say that they re-blog it.

And the conversation grows to include even more people.

The author's blog is a space that belongs to the author – unlike Facebook, Twitter or other social media. The author's blog is also searched and indexed by Google unlike the various social media (for the most part). This allows for your conversations to be searched for and found long after they take place. This isn't true of any material that you put on most social media. In fact, a post on your blog can be found years after it's created. The accepted shelf life of a Facebook post is considered to be between two and five hours and the shelf life of a Twitter post is 18 minutes. A LinkedIn post can have a shelf life of up to 24 hours in some cases.

An author's blog is the place where the author can share with their community; the place they can start or continue conversations and have dialogues. This is the place that the dialogue will grow a community of friends and supporters – people with like interests who will help spread the word about your book.

The content shared is based on the author's personality and interests and should be reflective of their branding. Yup – there's that nasty word – branding. We'll talk about branding – how straightforward it is – and how it's often blown out of proportion. We'll flesh out the topic of what to blog about, but first of all, we'll talk about why.

Why Do I Need to Blog?

THE QUESTION that comes up repeatedly during my discussions with authors – Why? Why do I need to blog? There are several answers to this question. At the top of the heap, blogging is a writing exercise, another opportunity to develop that writing muscle. The second reason is to communicate with your readers and develop a community.

We all figured out how to make friends in Kindergarten: "Hi, my name is Barb. Do you want to play with me?" As adults in the electronic world, the way to make friends is admittedly a bit more complicated, but not impossible. It goes something along the lines of, "Hi, my name is Barb and I write books. Let's explore interests we have in common and chat about stuff over a cup of virtual coffee."

The third reason, as I mentioned in the previous section, is to communicate and share with your community of readers in a fairly permanent way. Unlike the other parts of your platform, your blog posts can be searched and found months or years after they were first shared. So a post that attracted a new reader into having a virtual chat with you two years ago could easily be found today and have the same effect on a new reader.

Your blog is your public face to the world. In today's society if we want to find out more about a public figure, we "Google" them.

Frankly, we expect all public figures including authors to have a website of some sort where we can find out more about them and their books. As we'll find out in the coming chapters, it's important to have a blog, but generally not necessary to have a website *and* a blog. A blog offers an author the ability to add fresh content on a regular basis to their site – something that Google LOVES!

Think of Google as a toddler. For those parents reading this, you realize that toddlers don't stay interested in anything for long. Even shiny, new toys are quickly abandoned for the box they came in. Google is similar. Google is attracted to new content. A blog that's posted to on a regular basis provides a steady stream of "shiny new toys" for the Google search engine. This helps a site rise up the ranks in a Google search. While it's true that the majority of your traffic will initially either come from your friends or be referral traffic from other social media, you want readers to be able to Google the genre they read and find your site in a search. We'll talk more about this in a future chapter.

One last comment for this section is about tone and language. As I've mentioned previously, I feel that your blog should be a conversation – a dialogue with your readers. A blog post that's a dialogue with your readers is typically casual in its language and tone, like a conversation between friends. It's meant to share information as you would over a cup of coffee or a glass of beer with your friends. If your blog post is more formal, it will sound like a dissertation or even a monologue. It may end up conveying information to an audience, but it typically won't turn your audience into a community. In short, your audience will react differently. Think about how you react when reading let's say a Wikipedia page. You're looking for information and you get it. Compare this to reading a chatty, personalized blog post. You'll have a different internal reaction.

I'll continue to remind you to keep the word "dialogue" in your mind as we go through this book. I find when you think of something as a dialogue, that is what you create.

To continue reading, pick up a copy of Blogging for Authors from all major retailers: https://readerlinks.com/mybooks/733

WHAT OTHERS THINK OF THIS BOOK:

Covering the basics of blogging, with a spin for authors, Barb tackles each topic effortlessly, effectively, and efficiently.

Since I am a few months into book blogging, I skipped to chapters containing answers to burning questions. All of my questions were answered. However, her teaching generated new questions, which I am sure her blog and other books will answer. - *The Literary Apothecary*

Blogging for Authors was an honest, in-depth look at what blogging entails and how to get the most from it. I knew a lot of the surface elements that goes into having a blog, but Barb Drozdowich in her book really made me think about more ways to utilize and maximize my blog. Also how to be smarter with analytics and the advantages of linking up an author blog with Amazon Author Central and Goodreads.

There were great links and some video links in the technical section at the end. Pretty much everything an author needs to blog and grow their blog is here. ~ *Brenda Lou*

I don't remember how I came across this book but it is BRILLIANT!

I love the idea of blogging but seem to always get stuck to what to write about, and also felt a little self-conscious about it. But this nook offers ideas, tips and systems that help you to find your own voice and present a professional and engaging presence.

This book has really helped and I find I keep coming back to it every so often. Great for authors of all levels looking to improve their blogging. *~ reviewer*

EXCERPT FROM THE COMPLETE MAILING LIST TOOLKIT

INTRODUCTION

Welcome to *"The Complete Mailing List Toolkit,"* part of an ongoing series of author 'how-to' books, which is designed to help you navigate the technical issues of self-publishing. This box set specifically focuses on how to create optimized reader newsletters, how to grow your mailing list, how to ensure your newsletter arrives in inboxes and how to master email marketing services such as MailChimp.

I will use the word 'Communication' a lot in this box set. I feel to be successfully engaged with your audience, you must communicate with them, not simply bombard them with email and social media posts. Whereas many experts focus on simply gaining subscribers, I argue that this is too narrow a focus.

Why this book?

Two reasons: 1) This book is well researched and pulls information from many different schools of thought and 2) I take a holistic view of communicating with readers.

Initially, my intention with this box set was to collect information from a wide variety of sources and condense it into a neat and easy to understand package for you. However, as I was researching, my opinion changed. I found that much of the information available online and in various webinars seemed to miss the boat in terms of accuracy, while others just seemed fixated on adding people to a mailing list like hoarders would add one more item to a collection. They weren't looking at their readers as individuals, nor were they treating them as such. I wanted to create something more "big picture-ish" (is that a word?) – that looks at all aspects and all facets, of communicating with readers using newsletters. Hence the box set. For authors who just want to attack one part of this puzzle, the books are available individually, but my wish is that they are all read together.

I come from a background of technical training and while I'm certainly comfortable with technology, I tend to be holistic in my view. I want to break subjects down into manageable sections, and I don't want to skip topics because they are difficult to explain. I feel that I haven't done my job unless I can explain complicated things and make them relevant to you. I'm holistic in terms of looking at one subject within a larger context.

In terms of communicating with readers, I don't focus on only one part of the puzzle in this box set. I want you to understand why I suggest using shorter subject lines for a newsletter. I want you to understand why entertaining readers, is as important as communicating with them. I want you to understand why it is necessary to use an Email Marketing System right from the get go to communicate with readers. I want you to understand how to work within the laws that govern your actions when you communicate with readers. I want to explain why the technical aspects that many overlook are really important to success in your endeavors.

Most importantly, I want you to understand that there isn't a one size fits all method of communication. The way you communicate with a teenager isn't the way you would communicate with a senior. The material that fans of romance are interested in is not likely to be the same as fans of horror. I want you to learn what your audience wants, not take the advice of an expert without thinking about it and without testing it out. I want you to learn to talk WITH your audience, not AT your audience. I want you to see your readers as more than a wallet.

Seems like I have a huge objective! We are going to break the subject of communicating with readers down into four books. In the first book we are going to address the topic of gathering the names of interested readers. We're going to view it as something other than hoarding.

Next we'll learn to use MailChimp really well. There are many Email Marketing Services, but MailChimp is the most popular with folks just starting out. If you have already chosen a different service, note that the lessons in this section are transferrable to other services.

In the third book we're going to talk about making sure that our newsletters actually end up in the inbox of our readers. This book will be fairly technical, but you'll have a good understanding of why best practices are what they are.

Finally, in the last book, we're going to talk about how to create really great content that is appropriate for our readers. We'll bring in some science, some psychology, and some good old-fashioned marketing to help you form a plan for going forward.

I guess it is too soon to say that I've really enjoyed writing these books…but I hope that you appreciate my efforts and learn to be better communicators with your readers!

Onward…

To continue reading, grab a copy of this book from other online retailers: https://readerlinks.com/mybooks/733

WHAT OTHERS ARE SAYING ABOUT THIS BOOK:

Drozdowich gives the "why" and the "how" of MailChimp's functions, and, even more helpful, shows what she uses or does not use (and why). This is so much better than the "you should" lists of some guides. ~ *Kay from Seattle*

Ms Drozdowich has an impressive portfolio of author related "how to …" books and a well-deserved loyal following. With this latest offering, she provides help navigating this extremely important book marketing tool.
~ *James Minter*

It's comprehensive, it's detailed, it's accessible to read. It makes complex technicalities easy to understand. It's an extensive how-to set of books for those who want to build a mailing list and establish quality relationships with their readers through newsletters. ~ *Ana T*